FOOD COLORING BOOK

- - -

DELICIOUSLY SCRUMPTIOUS

CUP-CAKES

&

PSYCHEDELIC STRESS-RELIEVING

FOOD

- - -

COLORING BOOK FOR ADULTS

2 BOOK BUNDLE

DELICIOUSLY SCRUMPTIOUS CUP-CAKES

Food Coloring Book

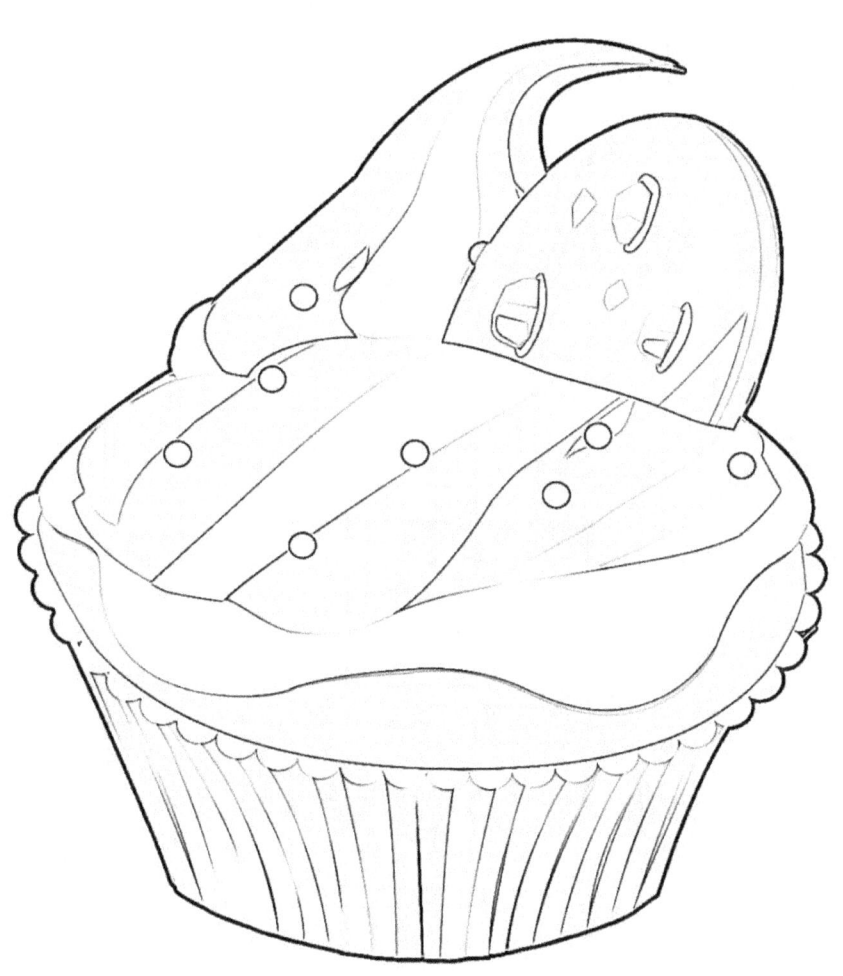

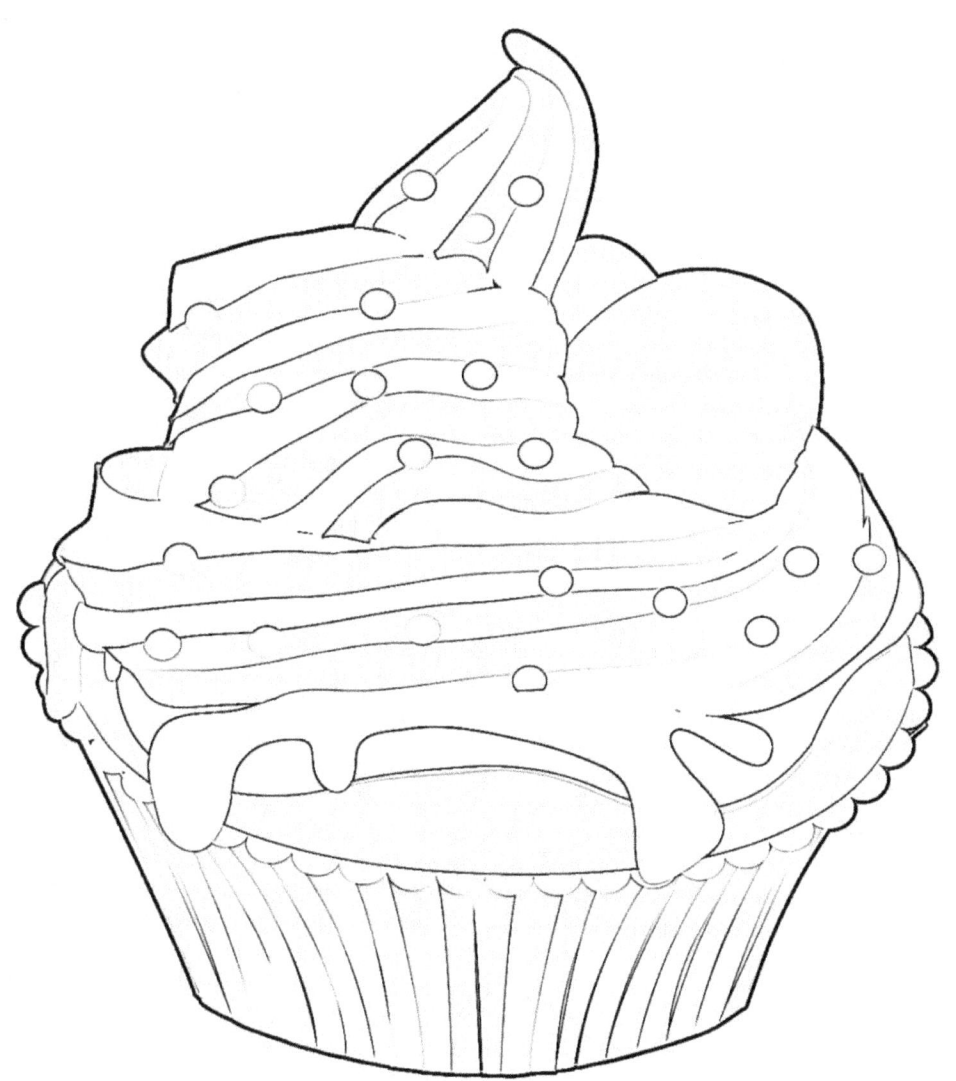

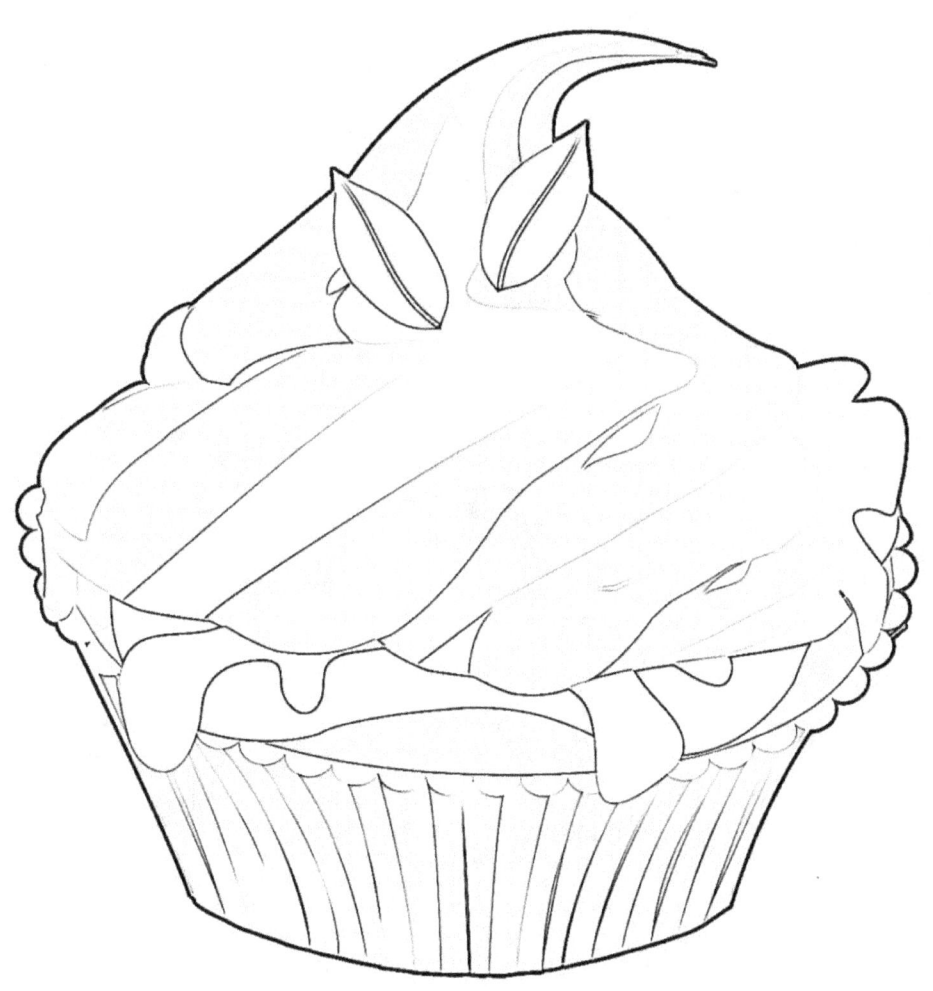

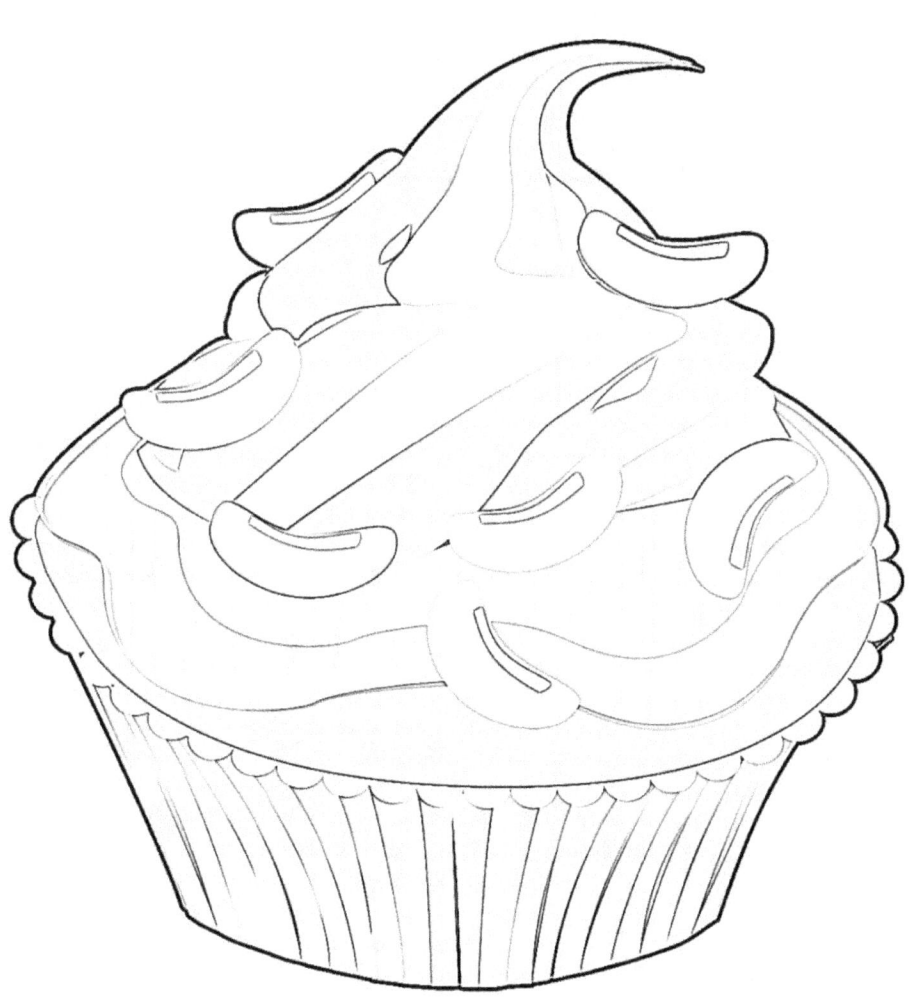

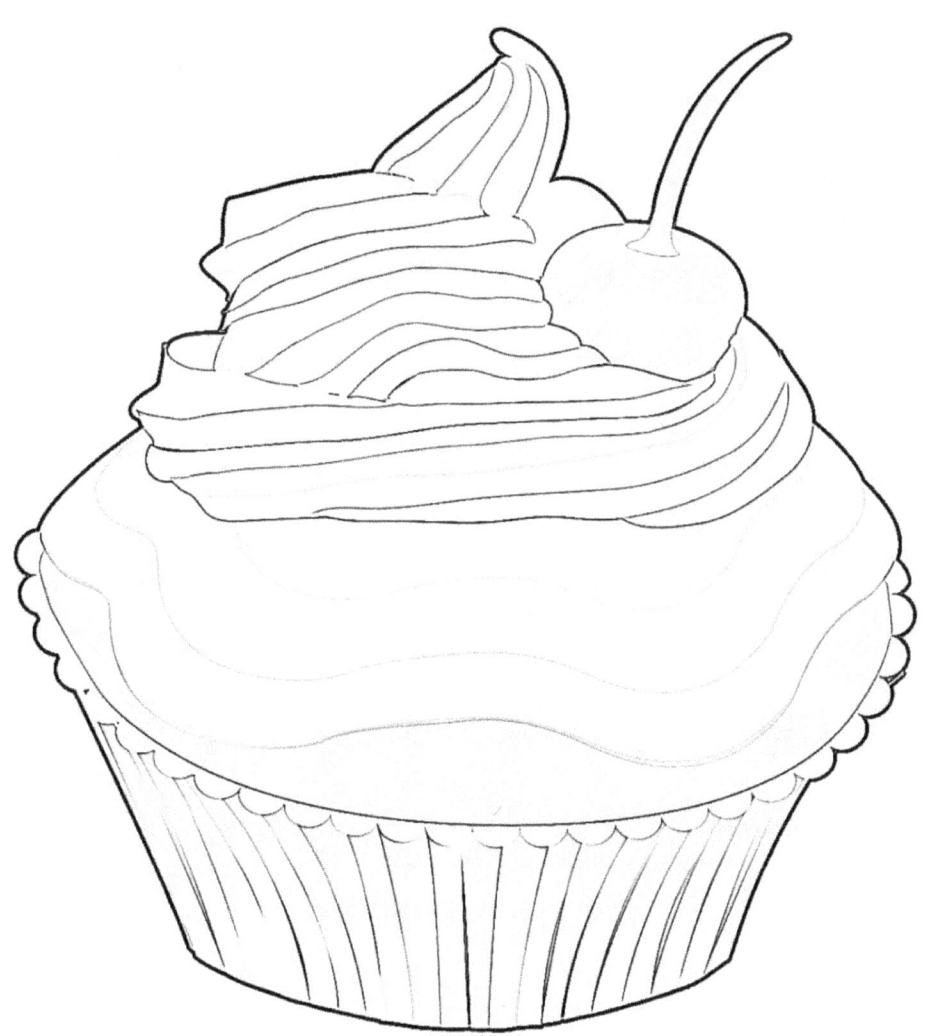

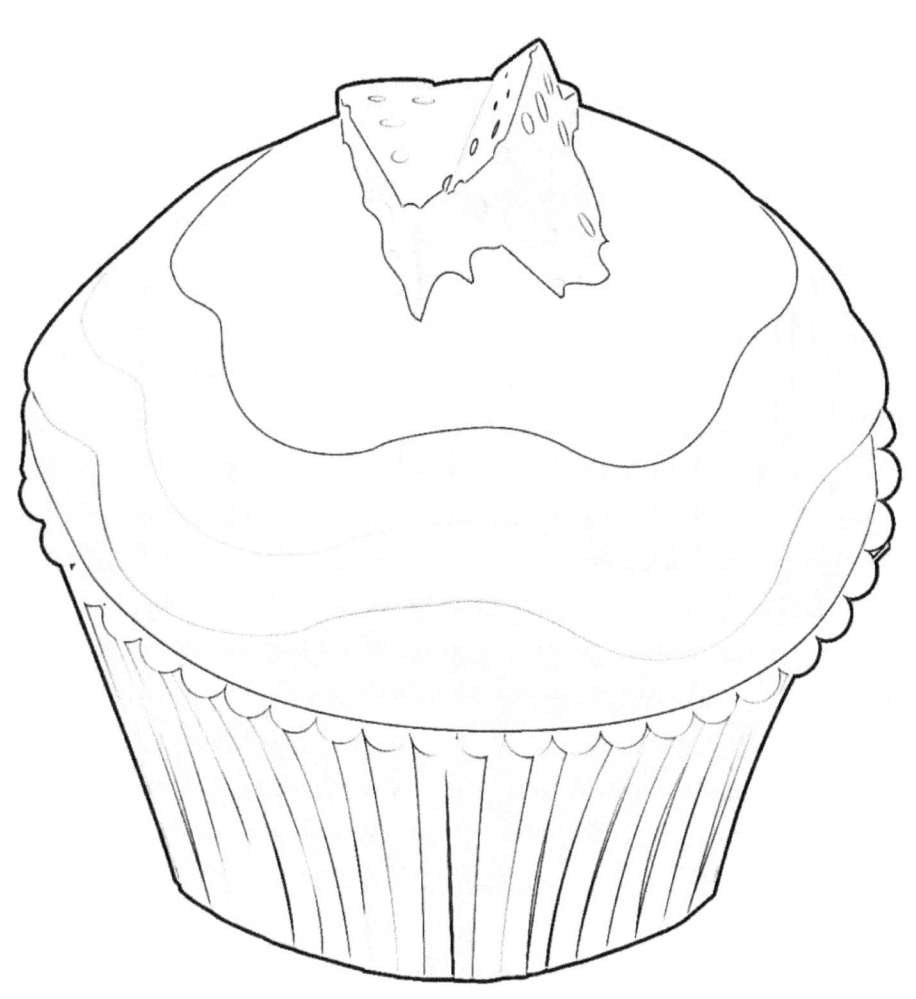

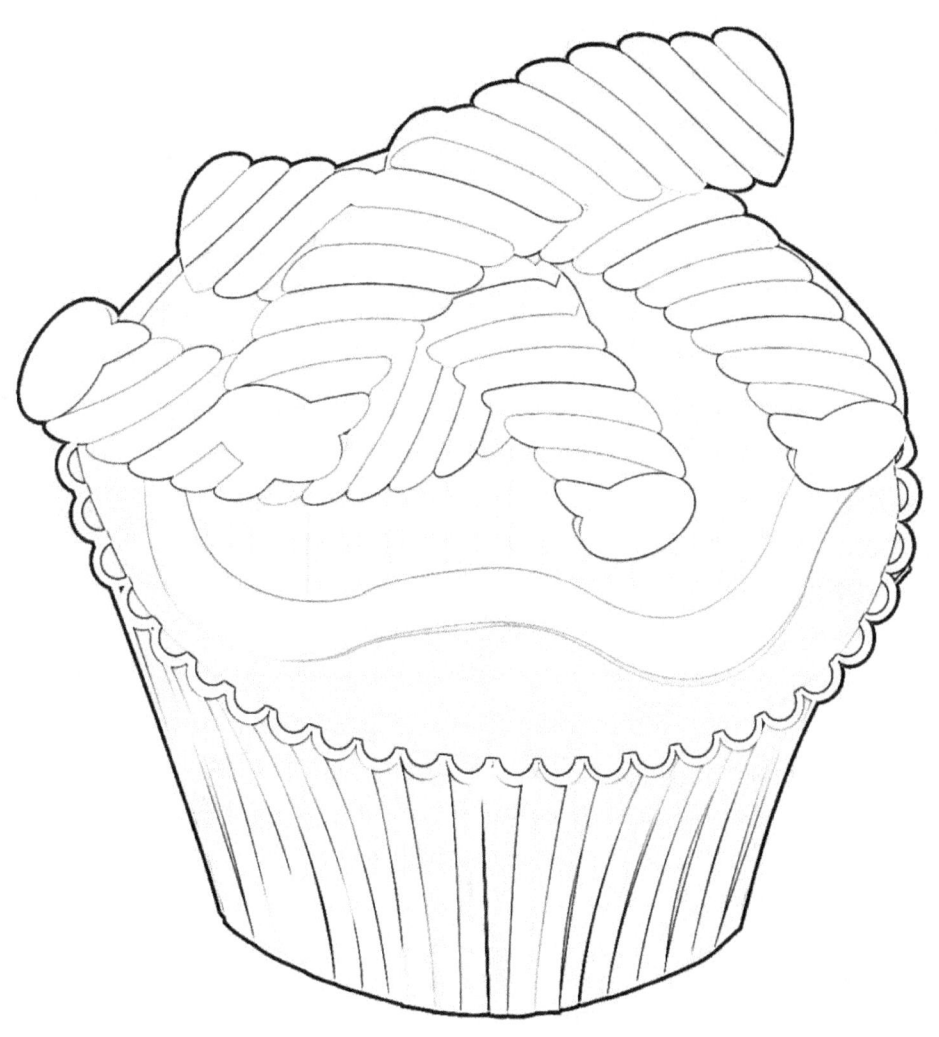

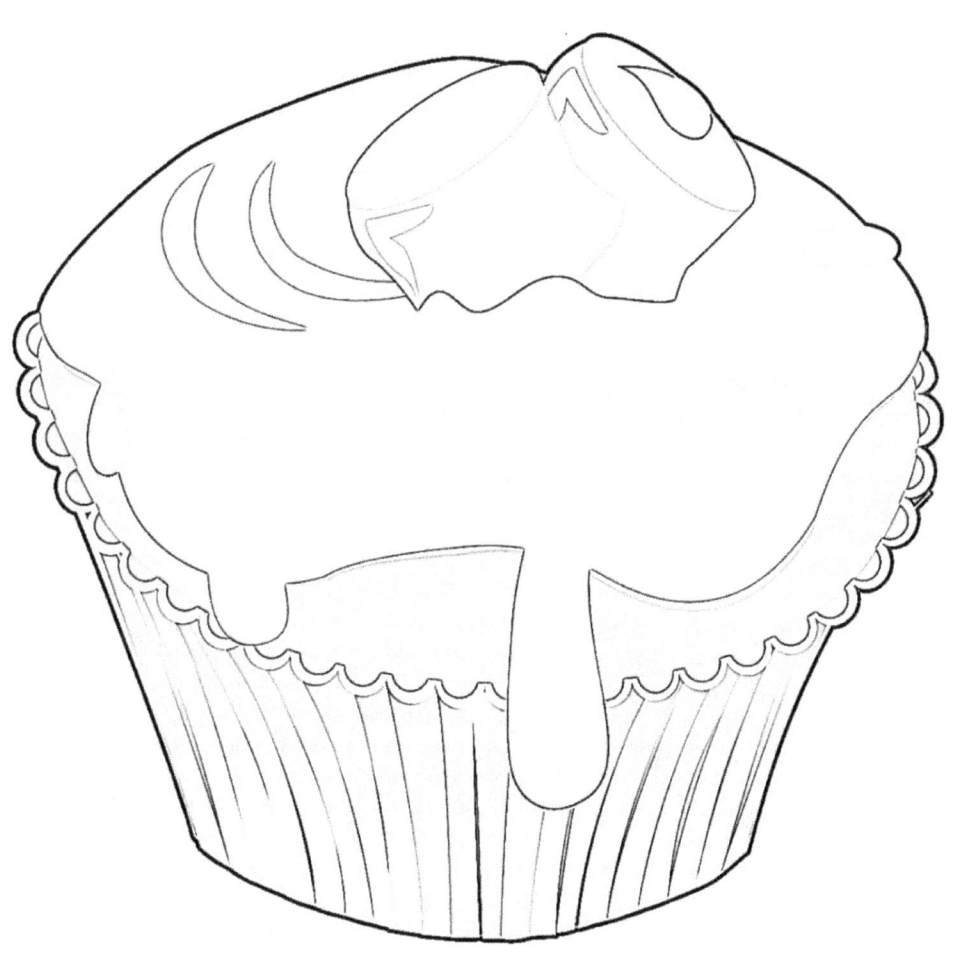

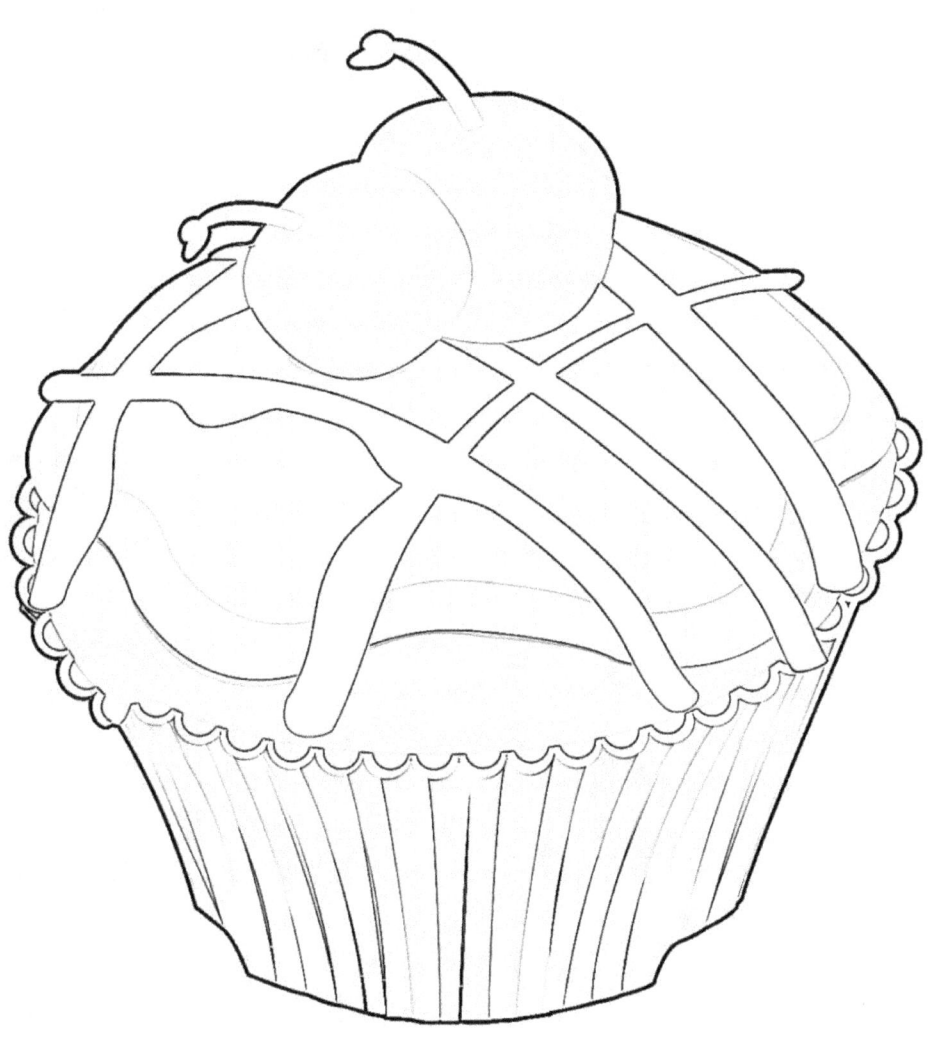

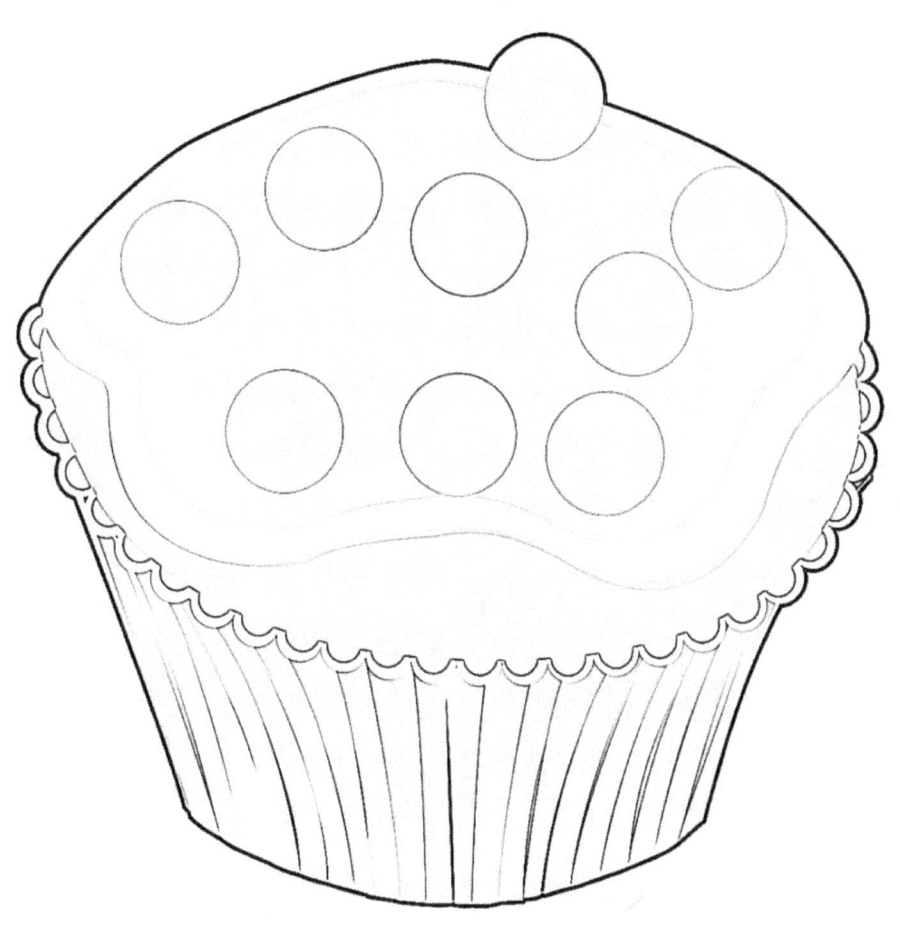

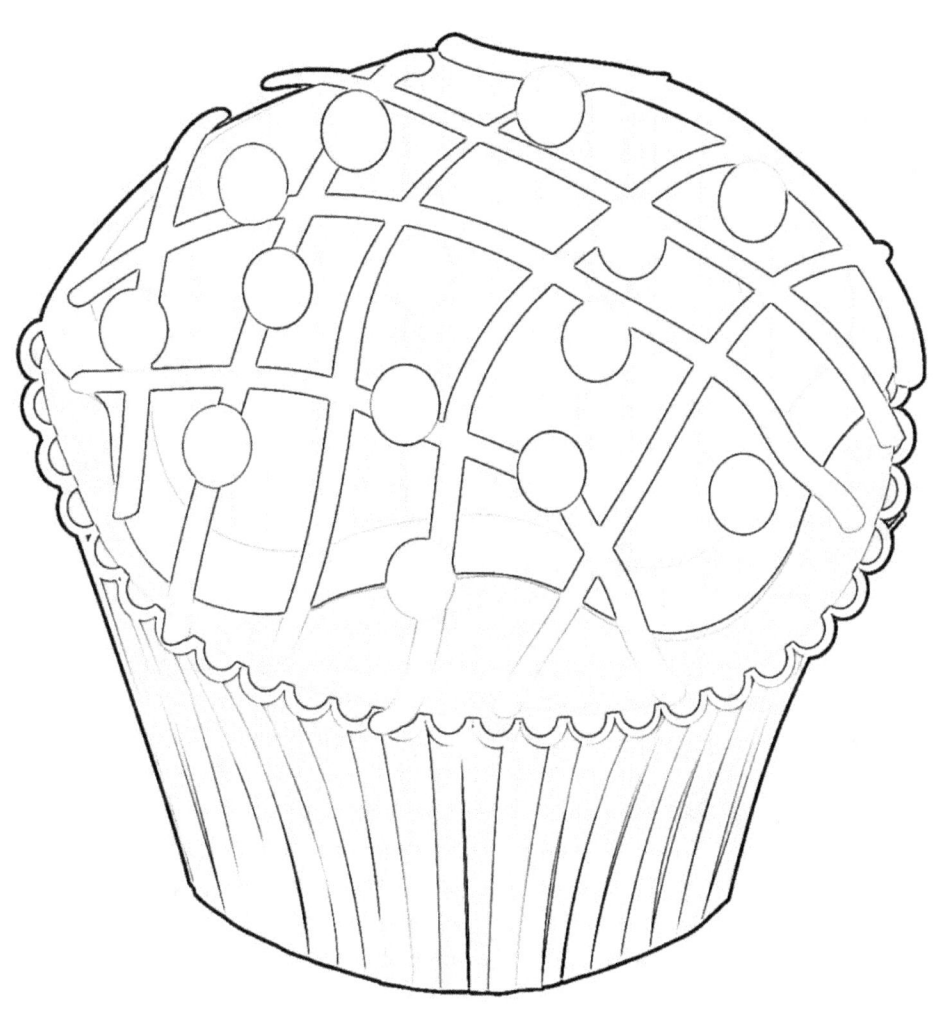

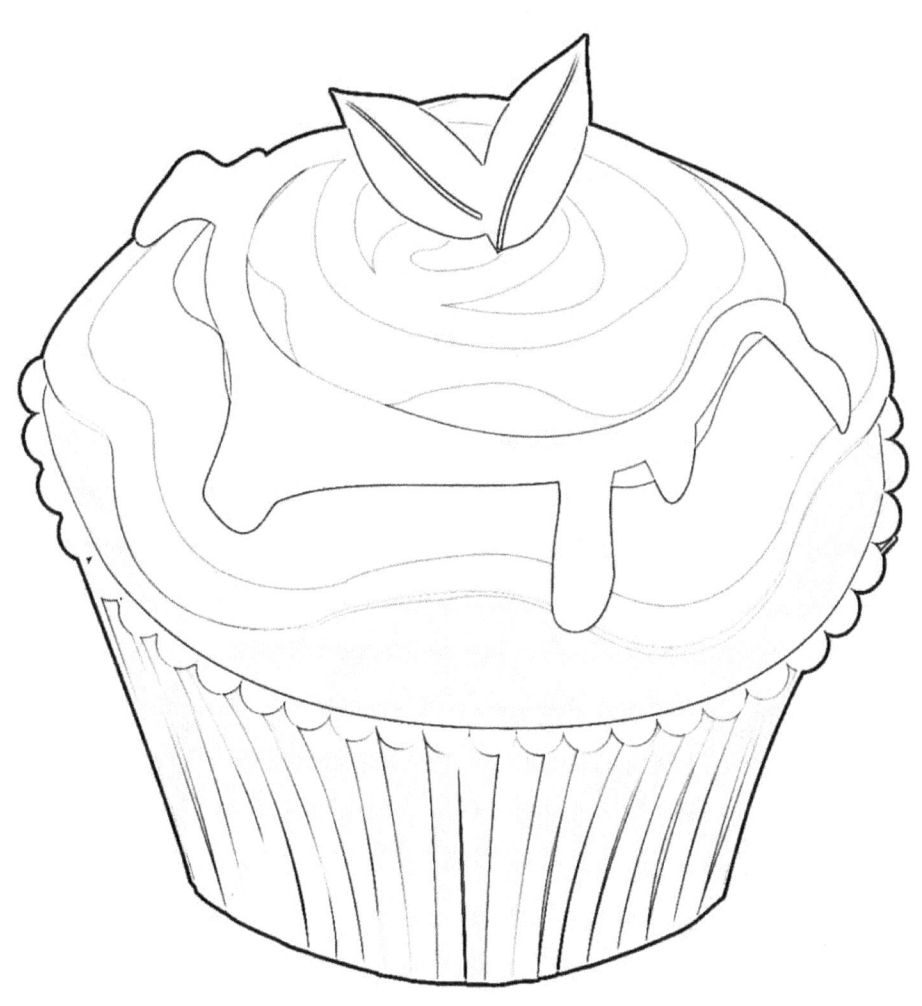

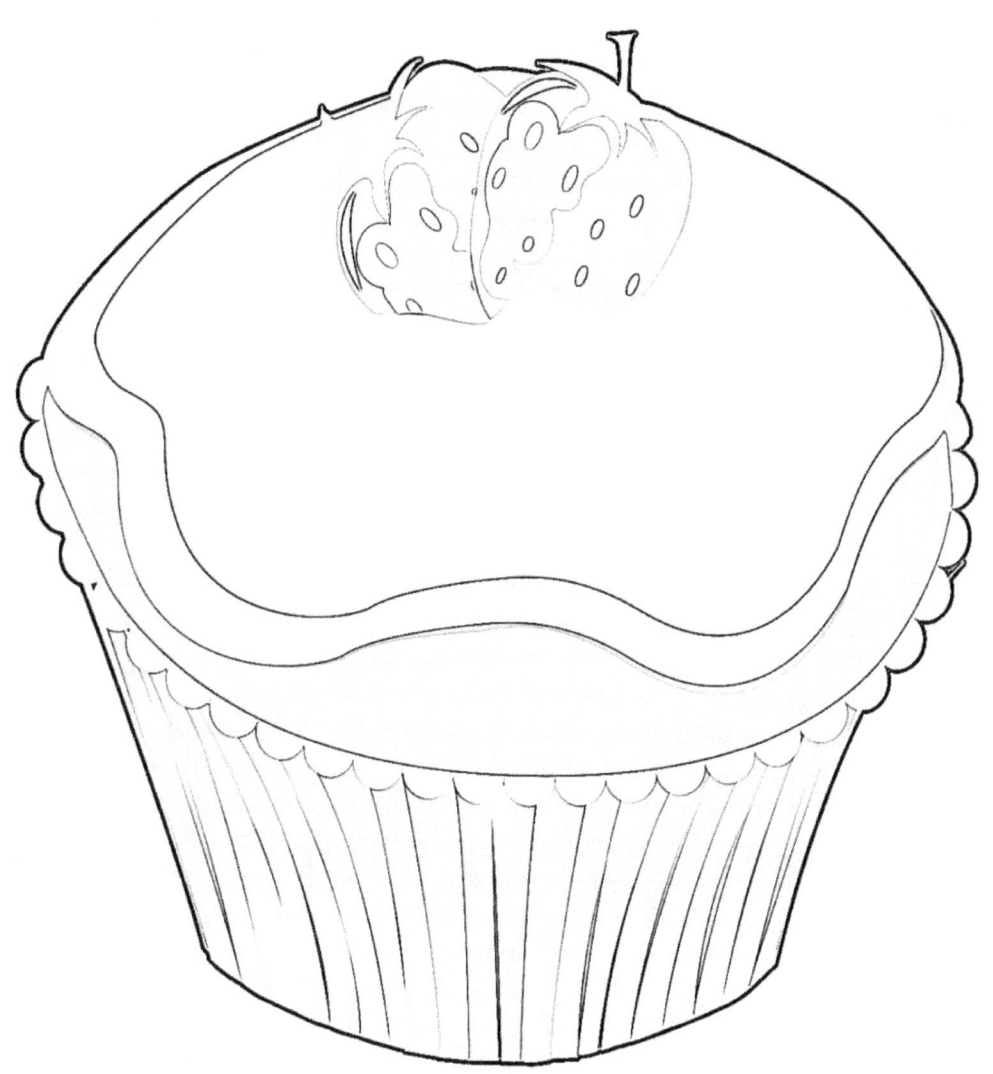

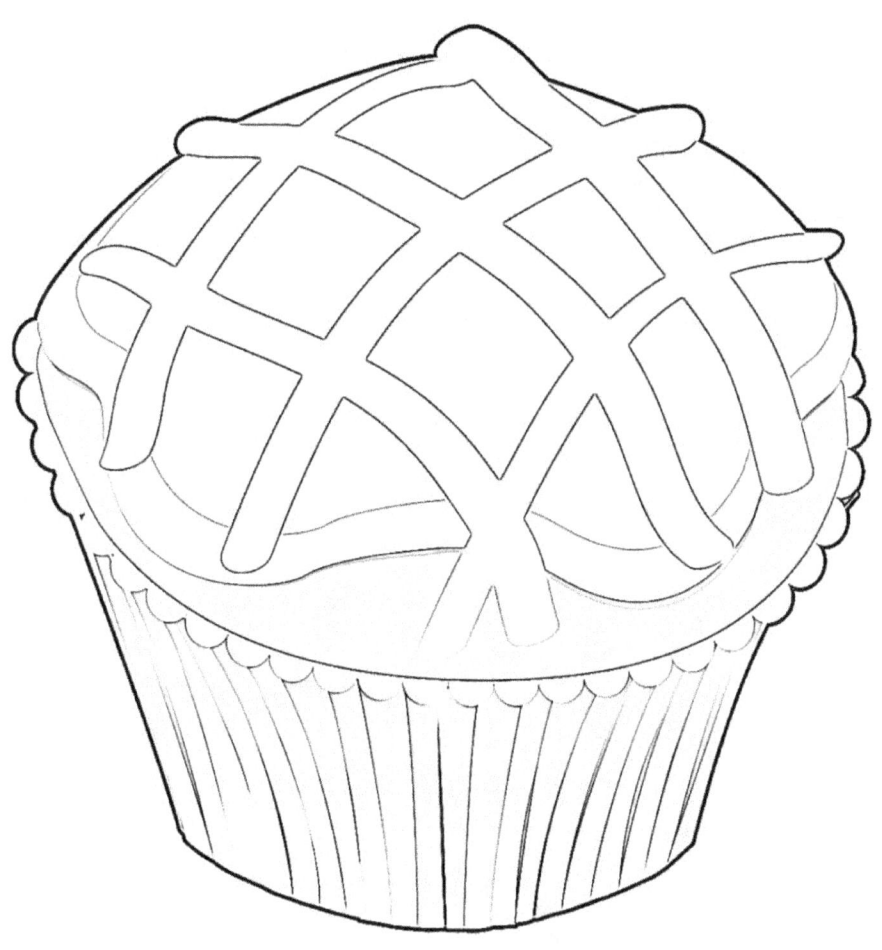

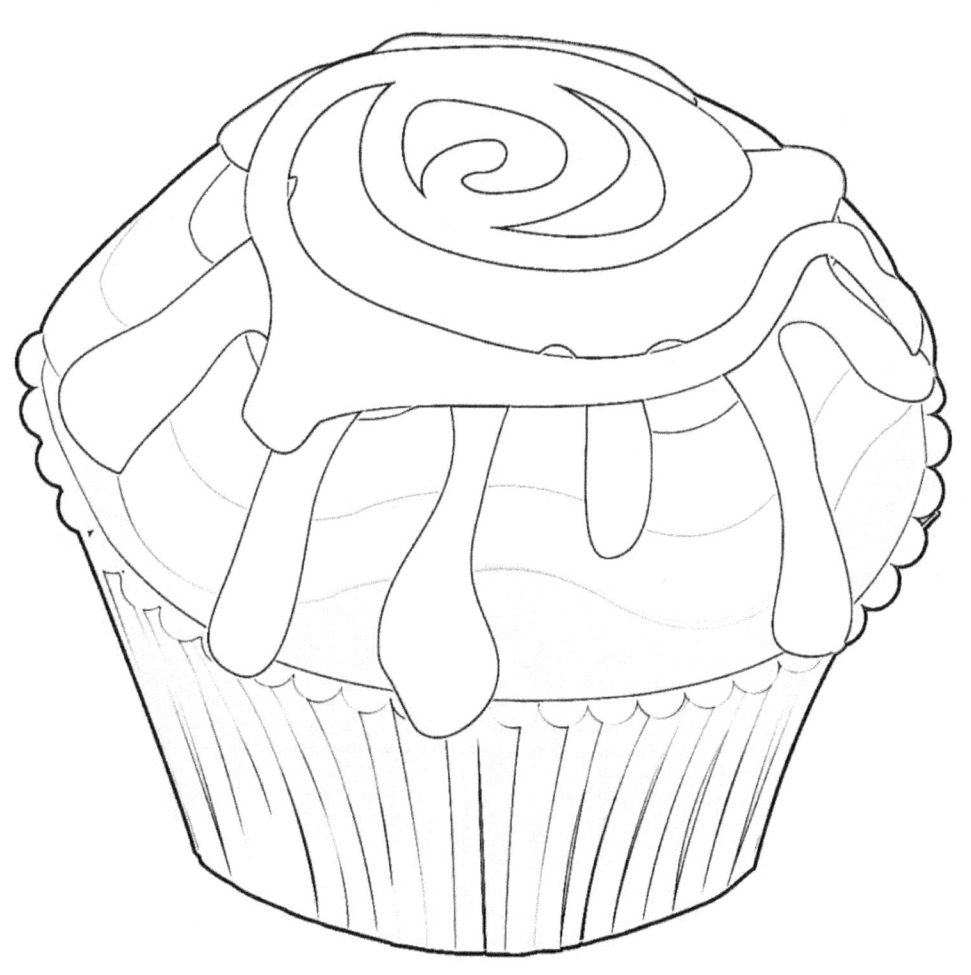

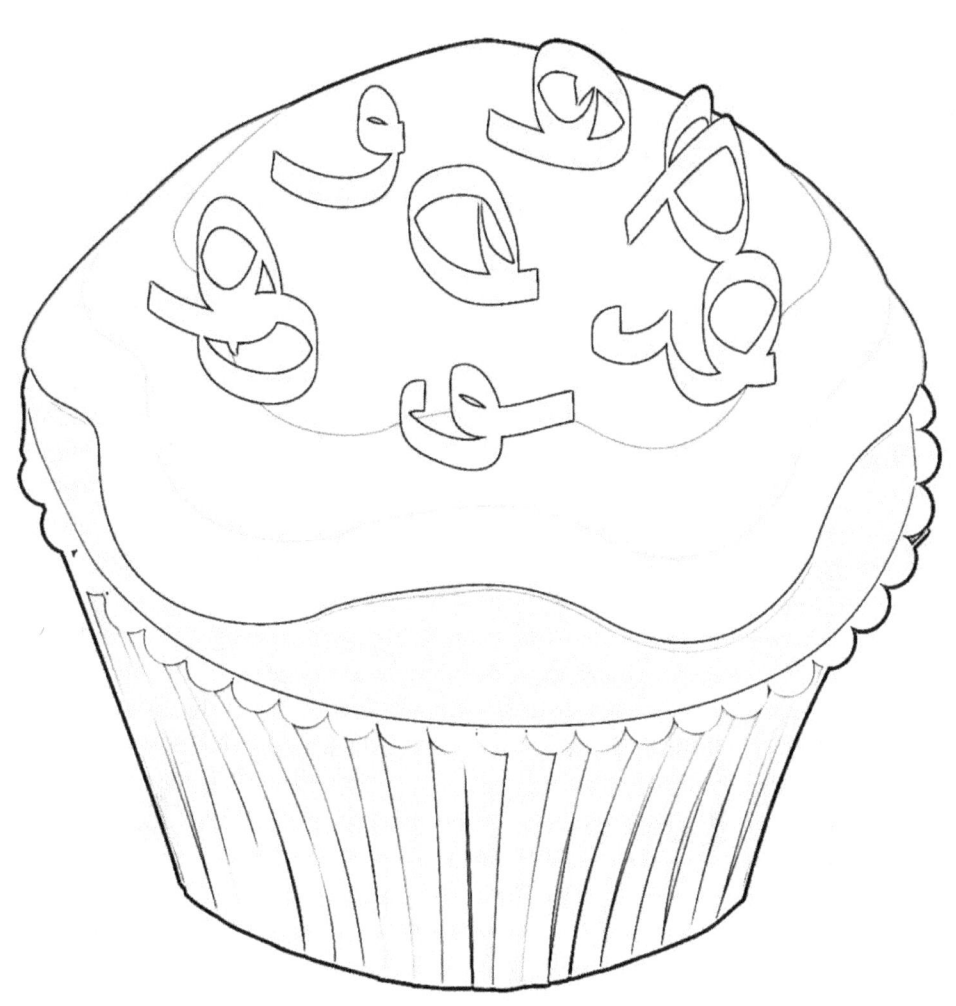

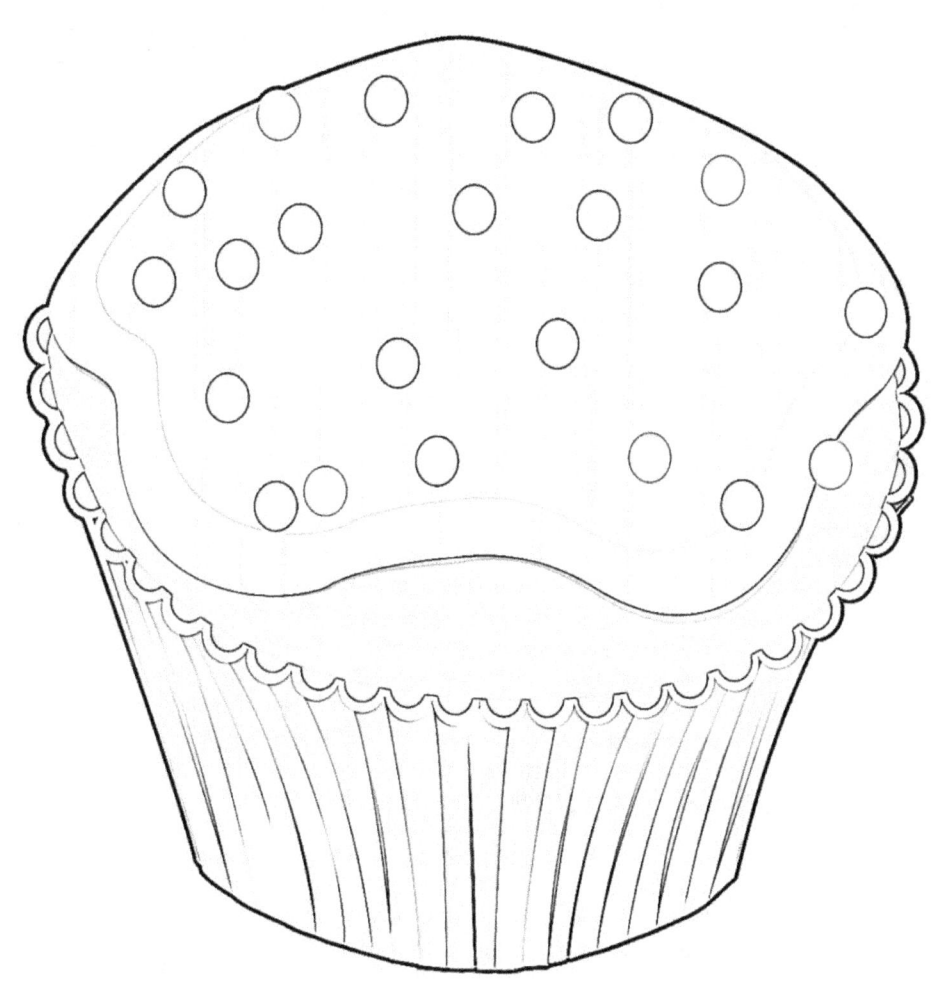

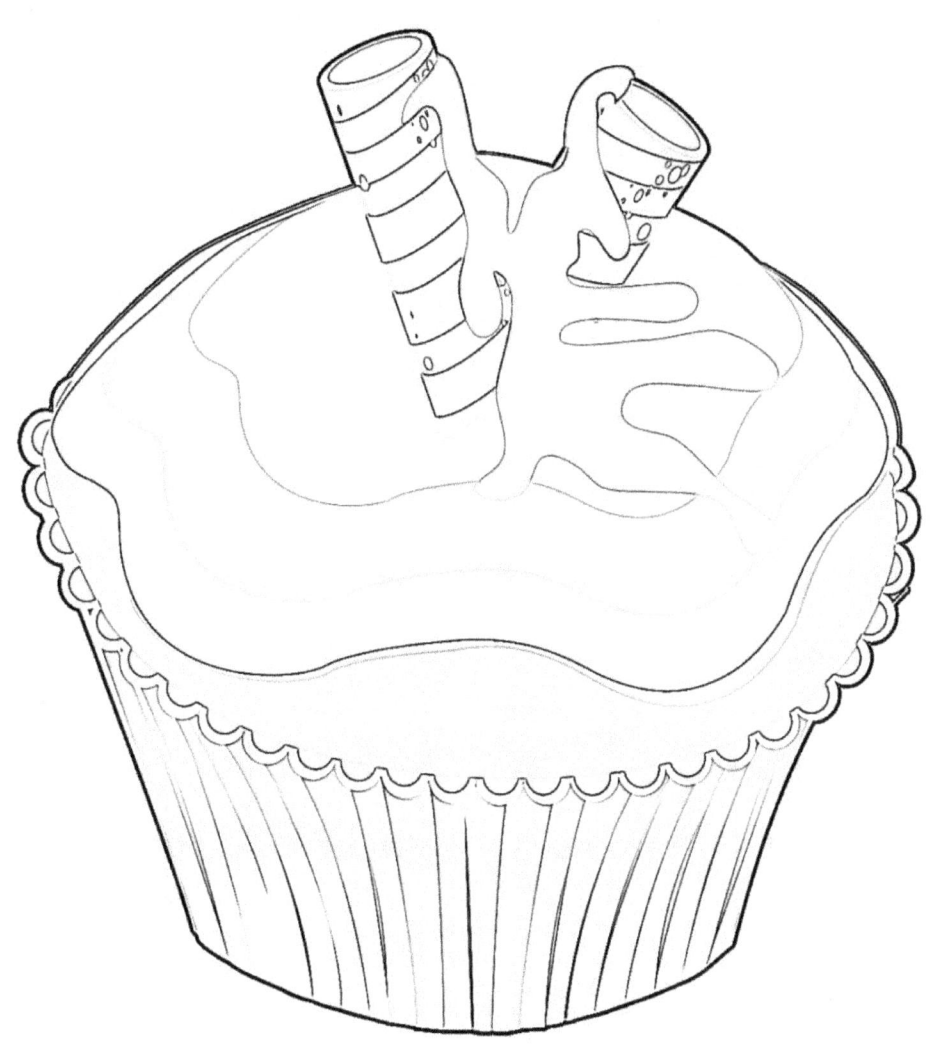

Food Coloring Book

PSYCHEDELIC
STRESS-RELIEVING FOOD

A Coloring Book For Adults

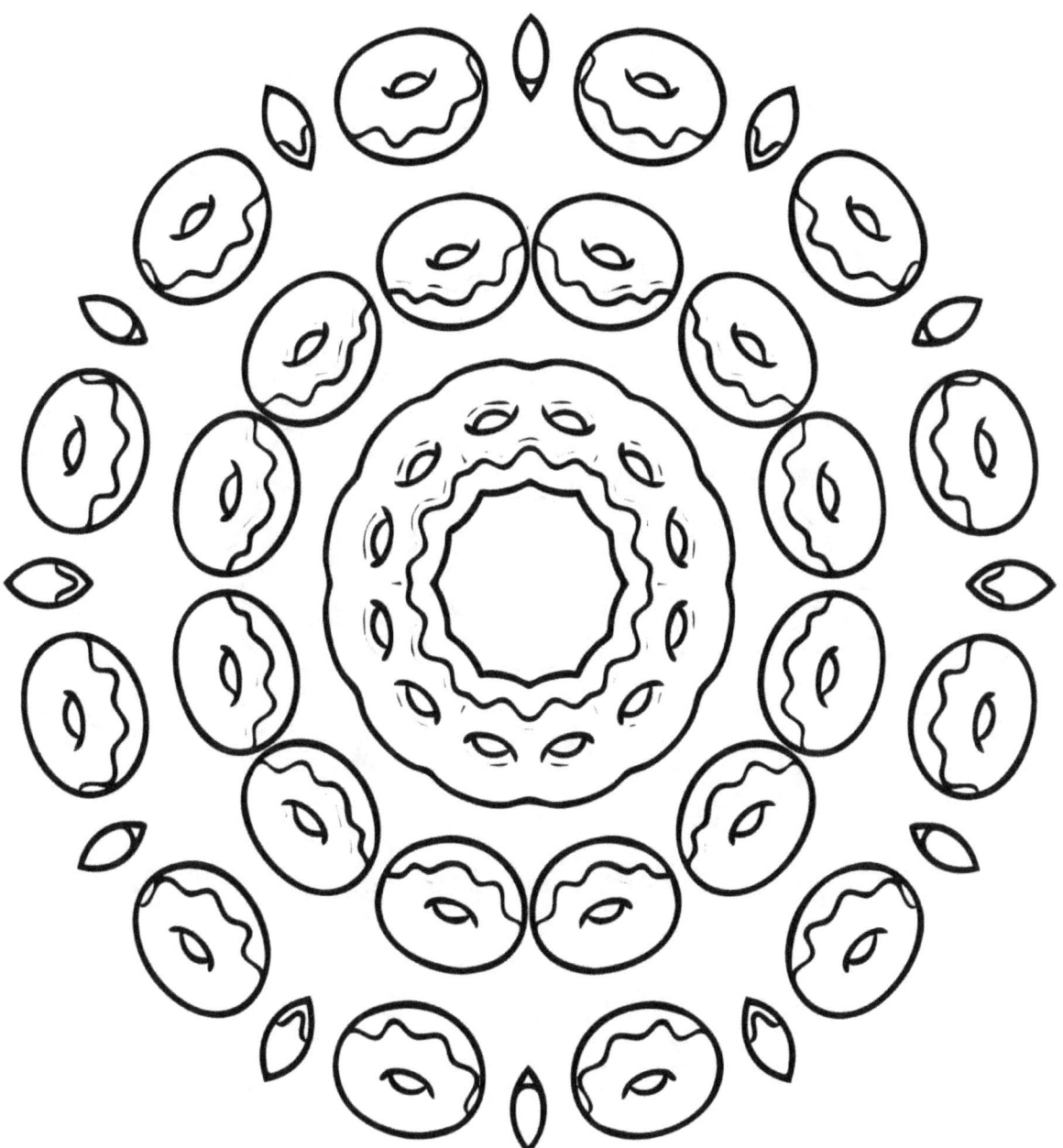

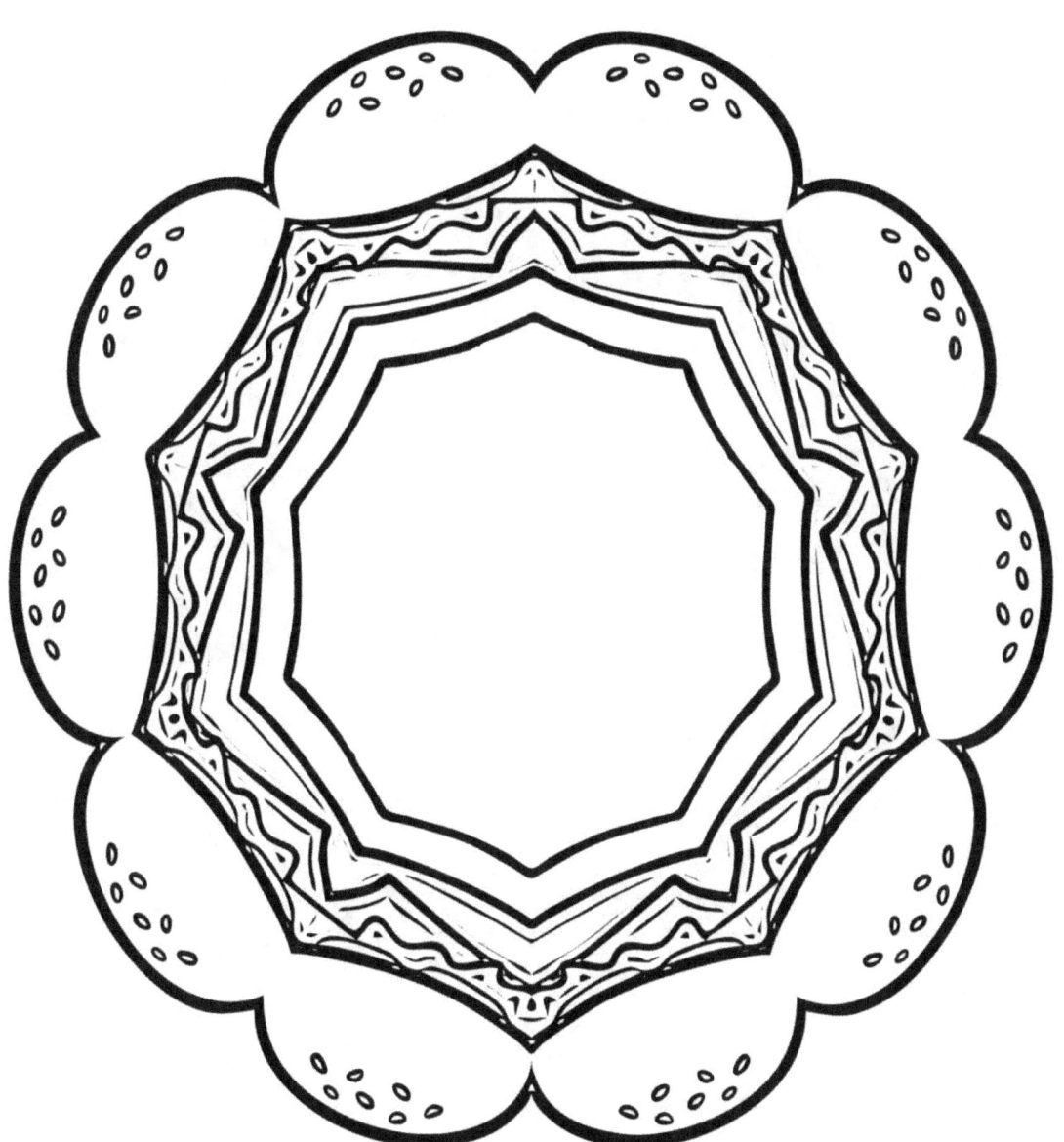

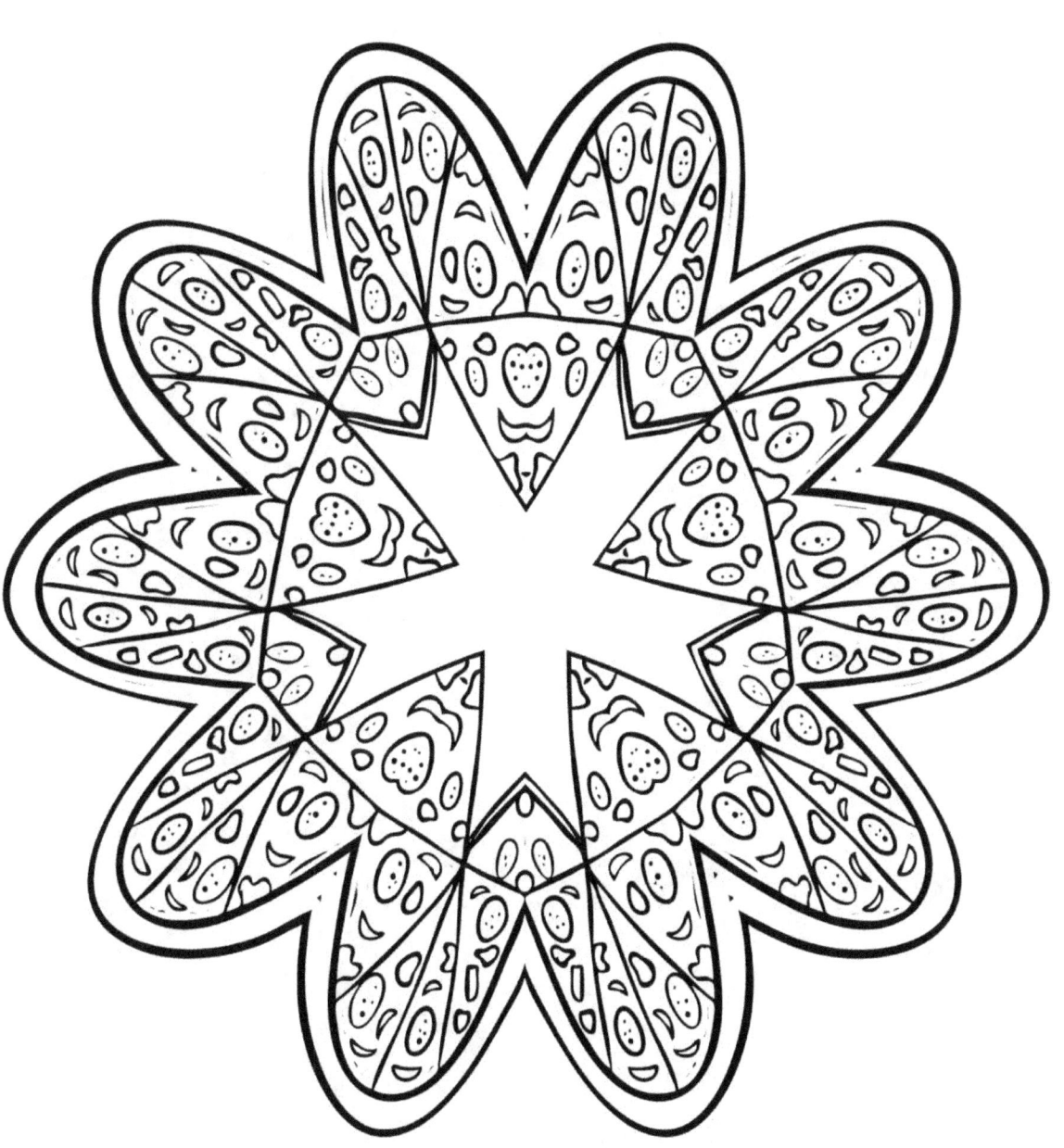

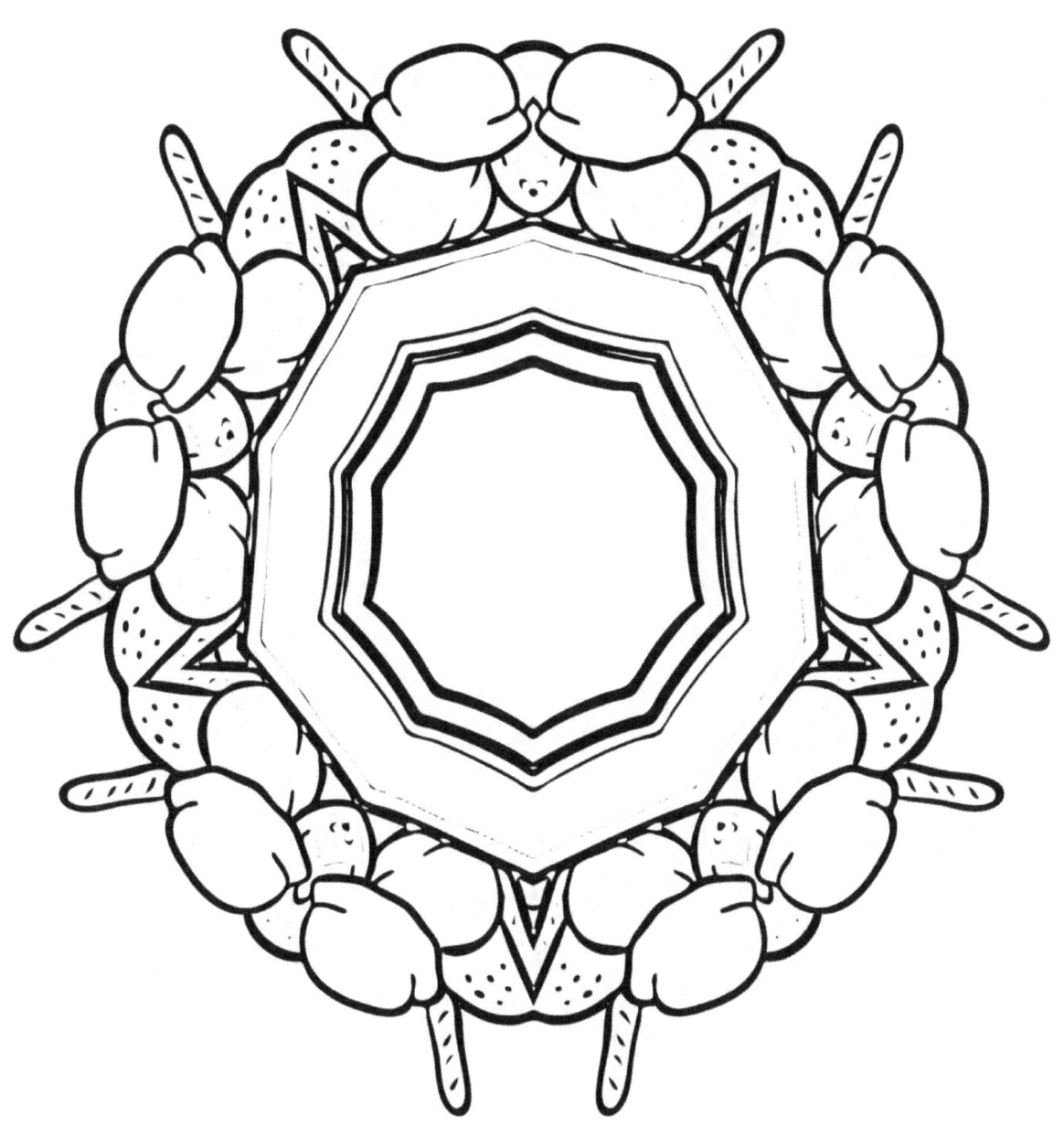

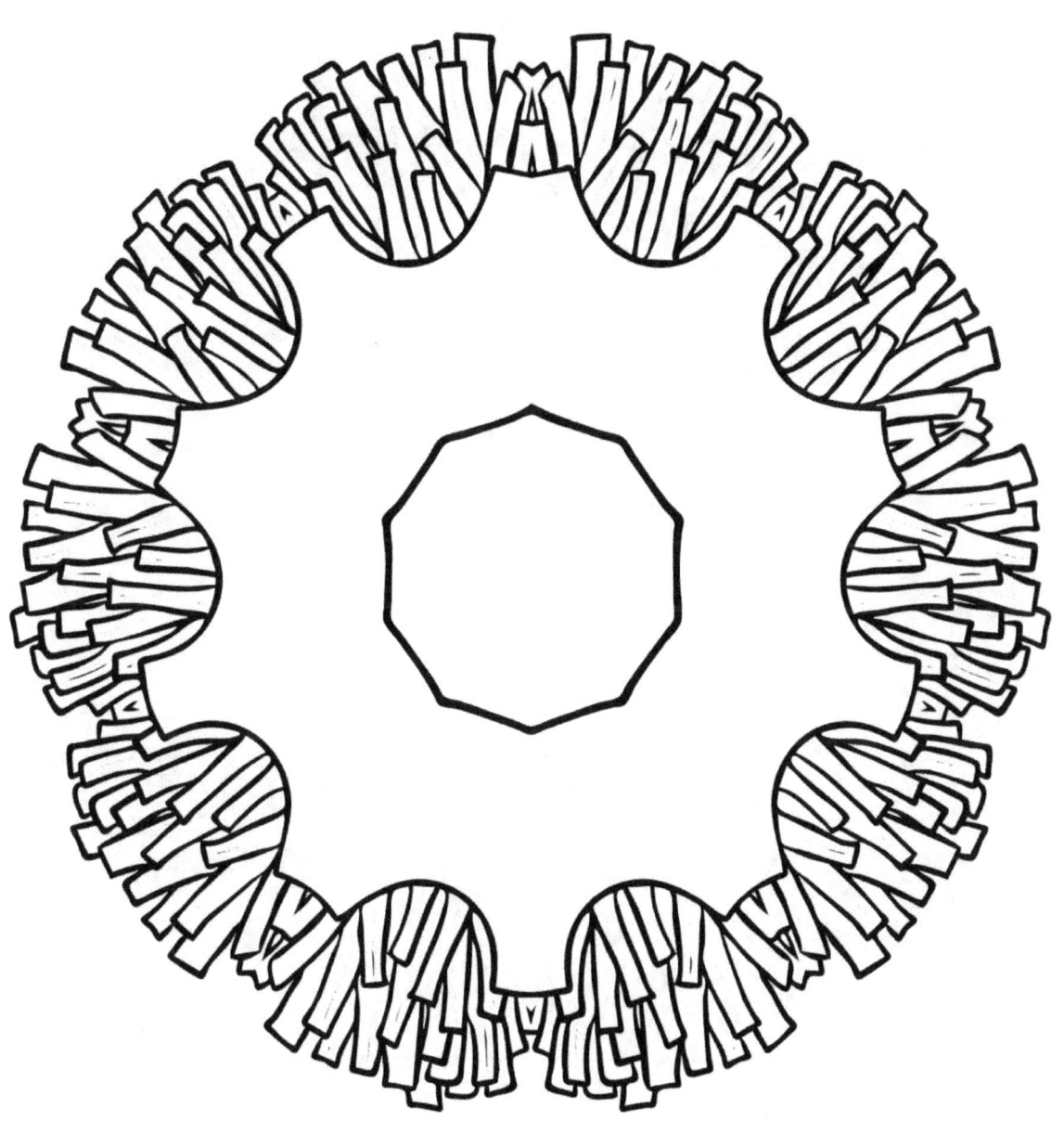

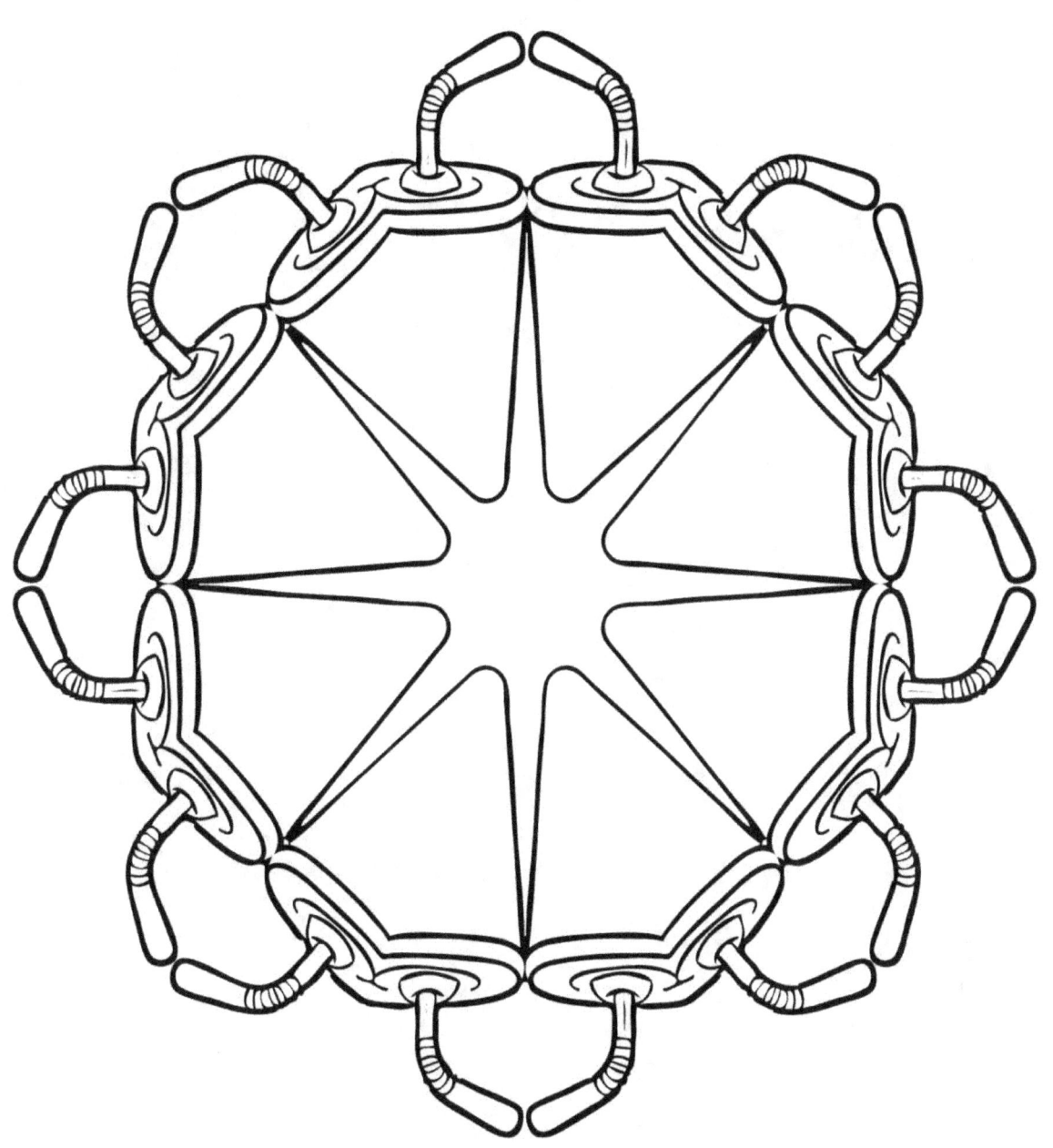

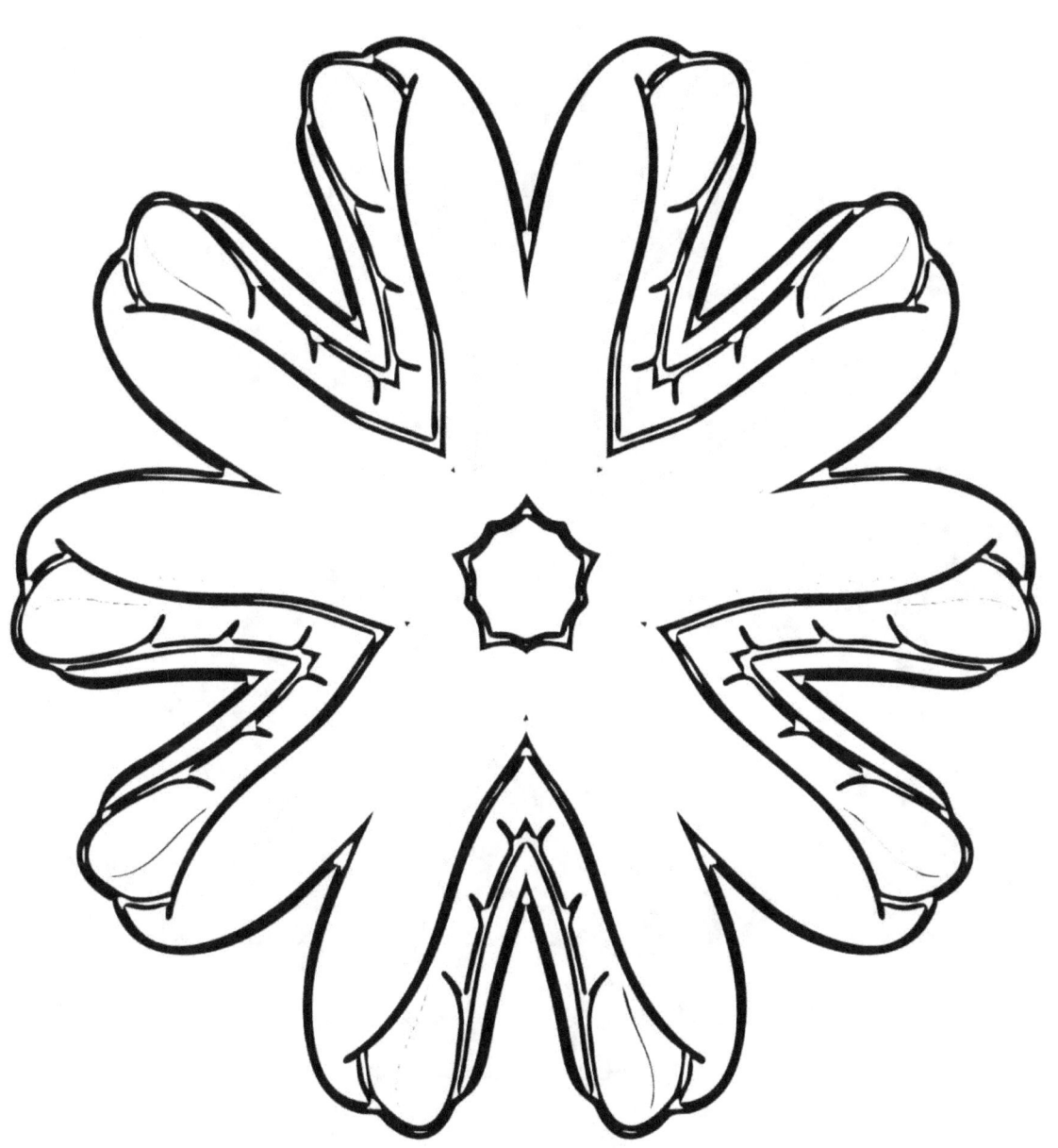

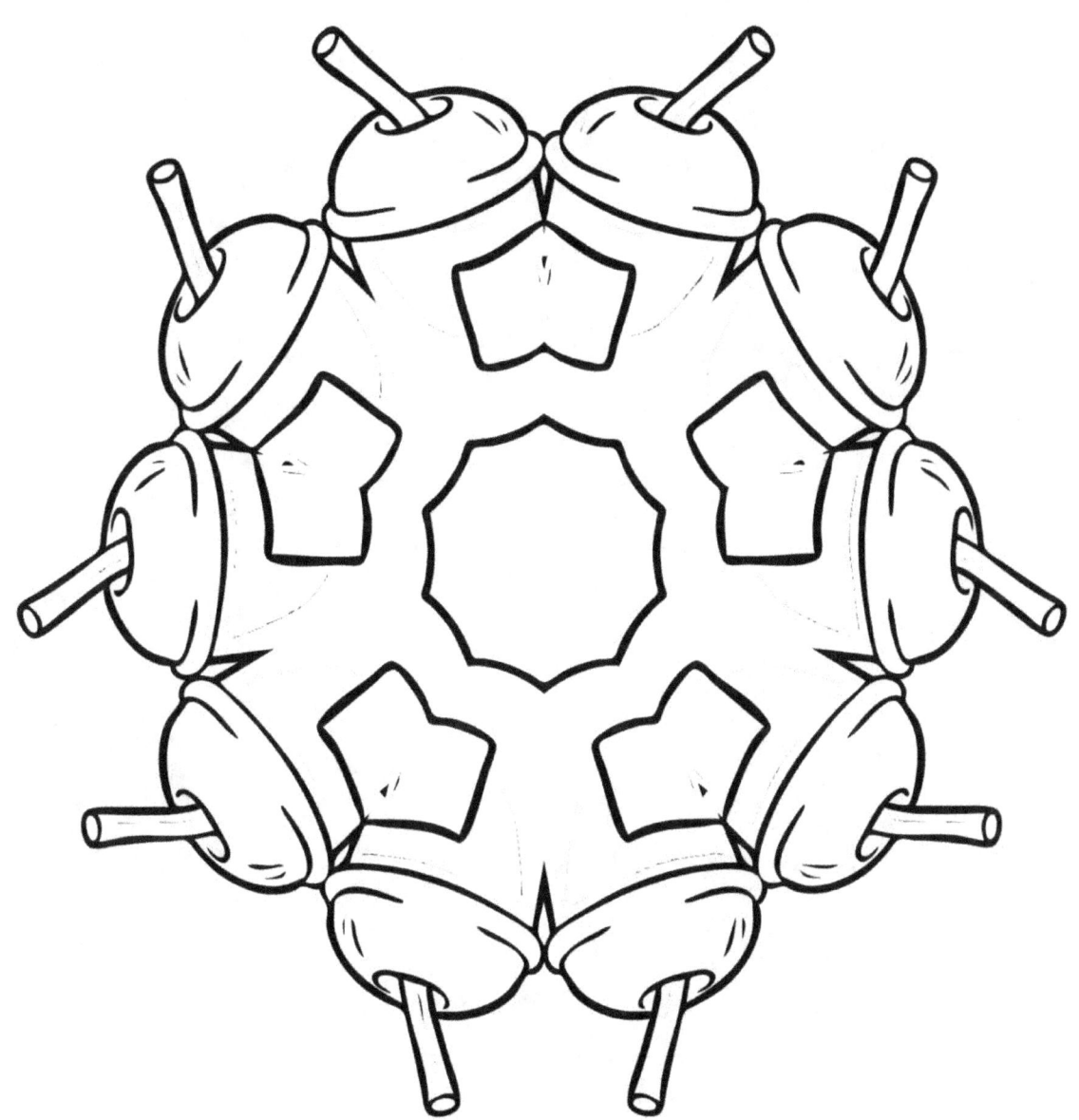

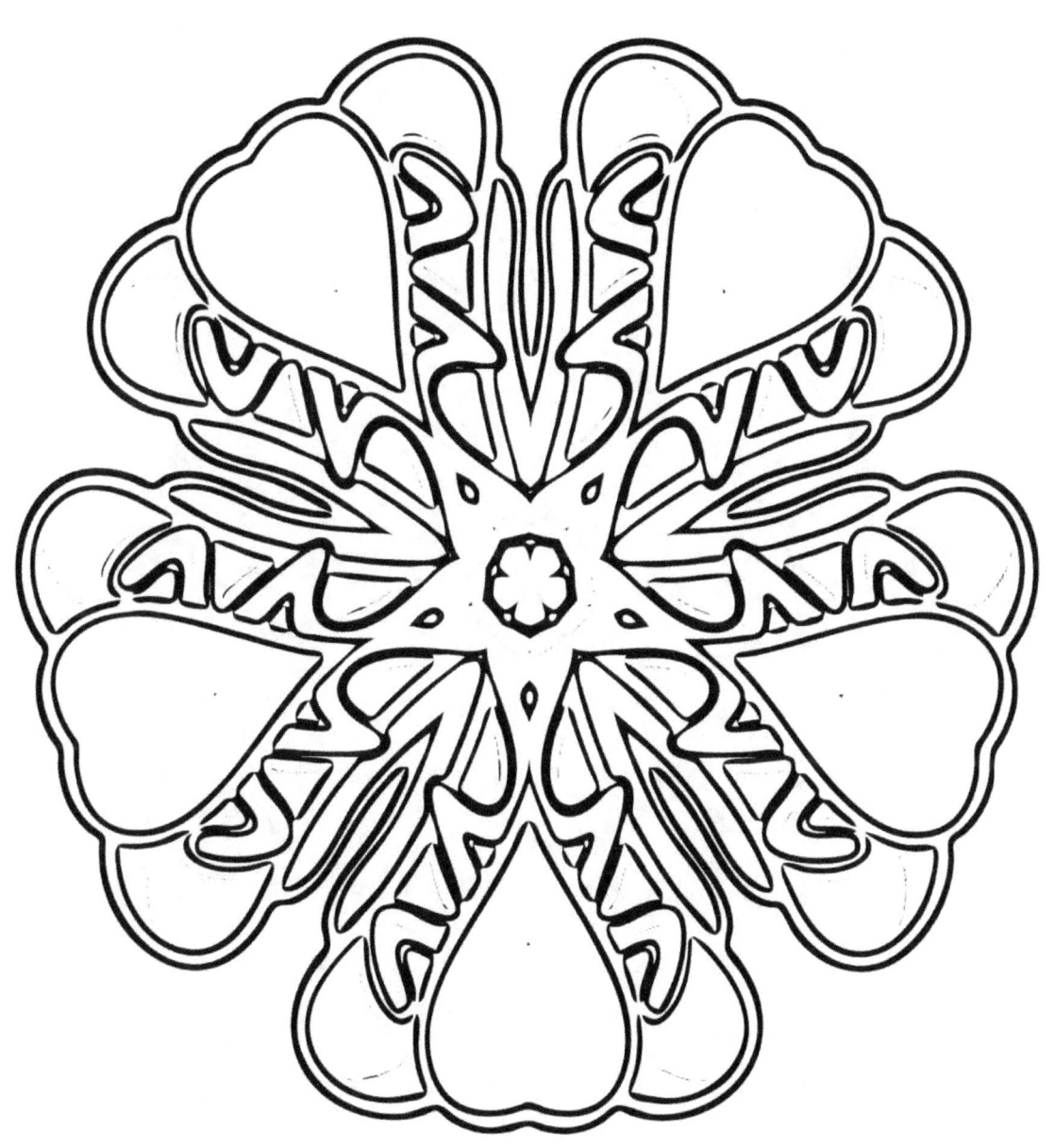

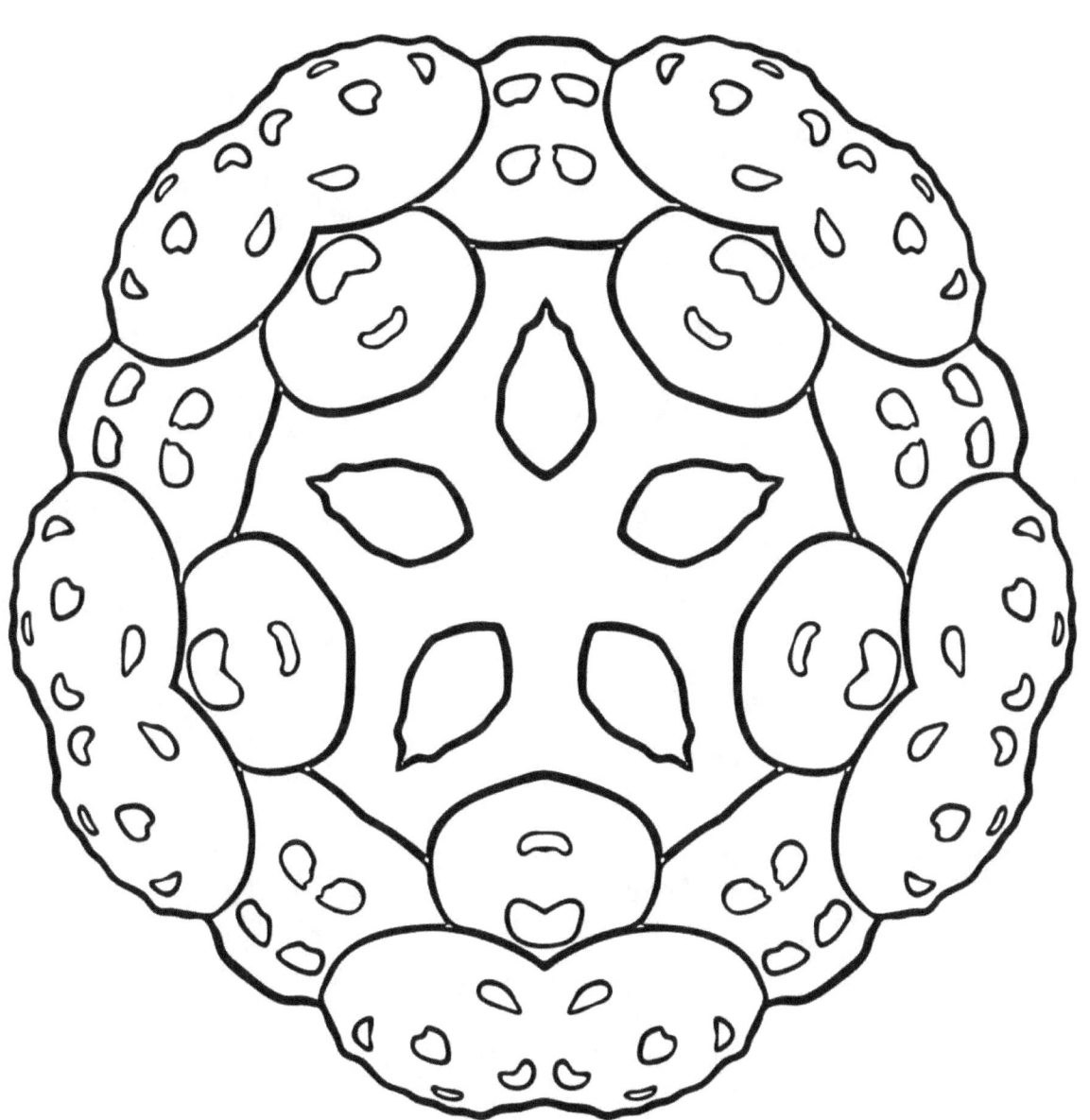

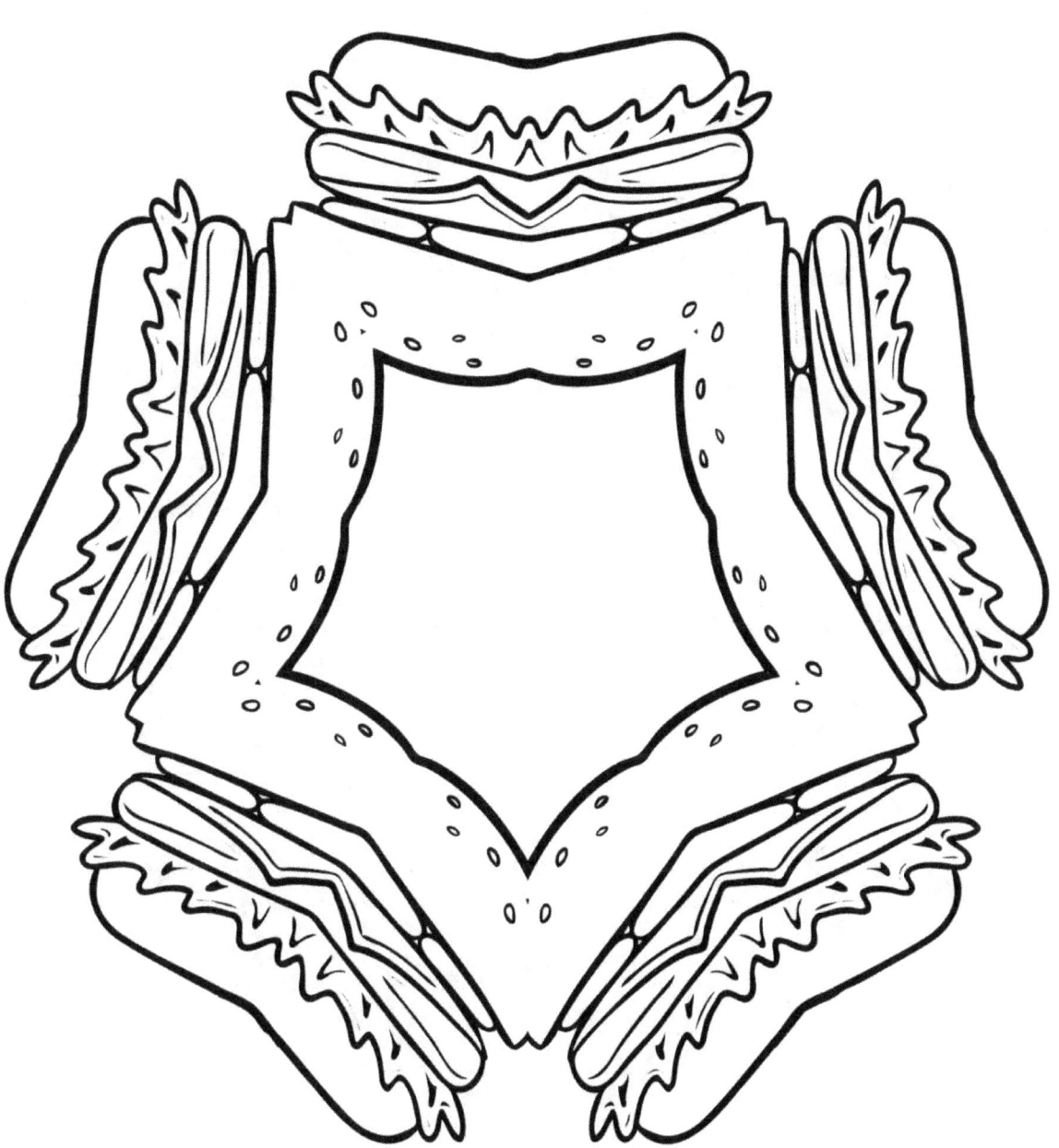

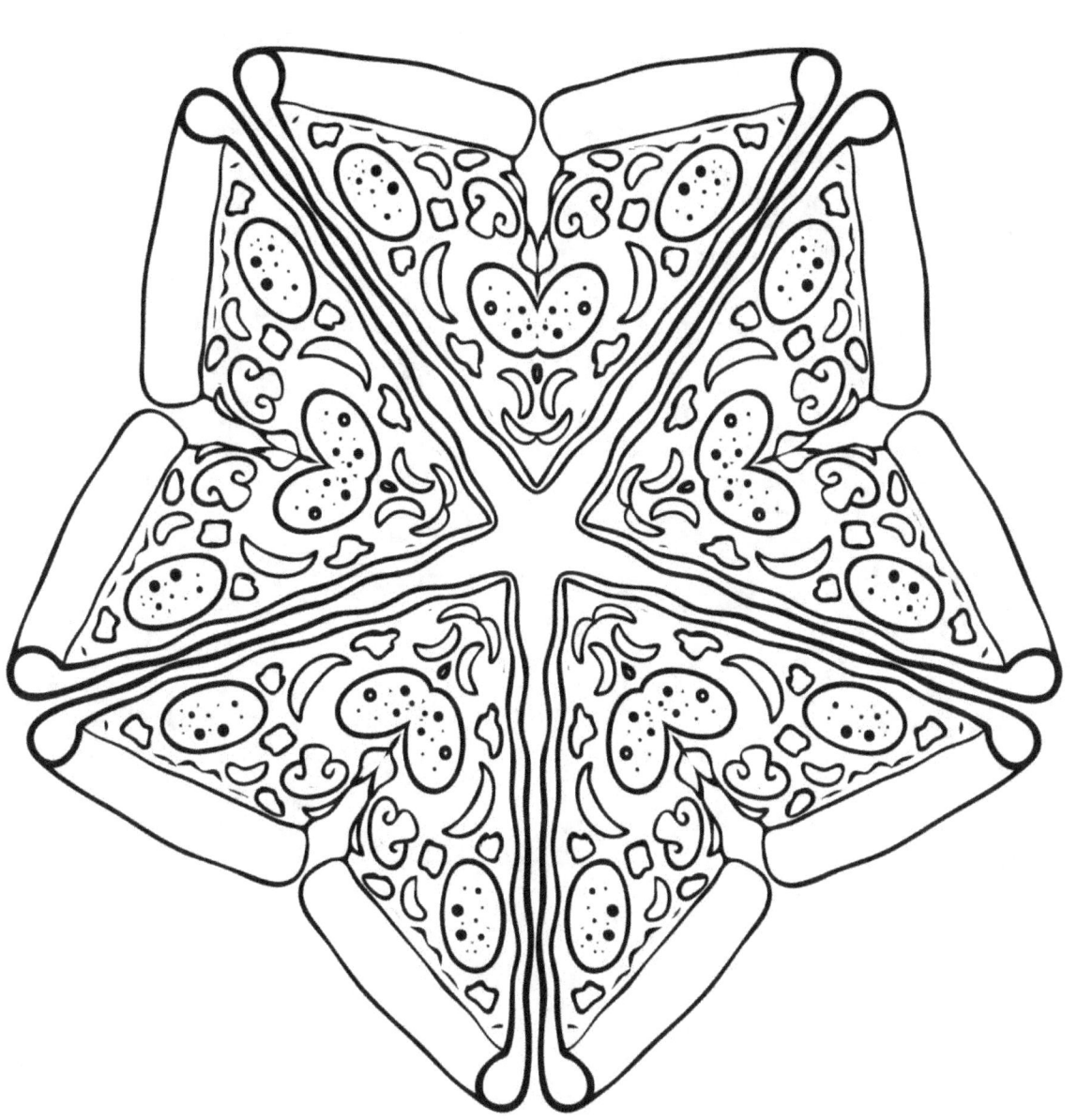

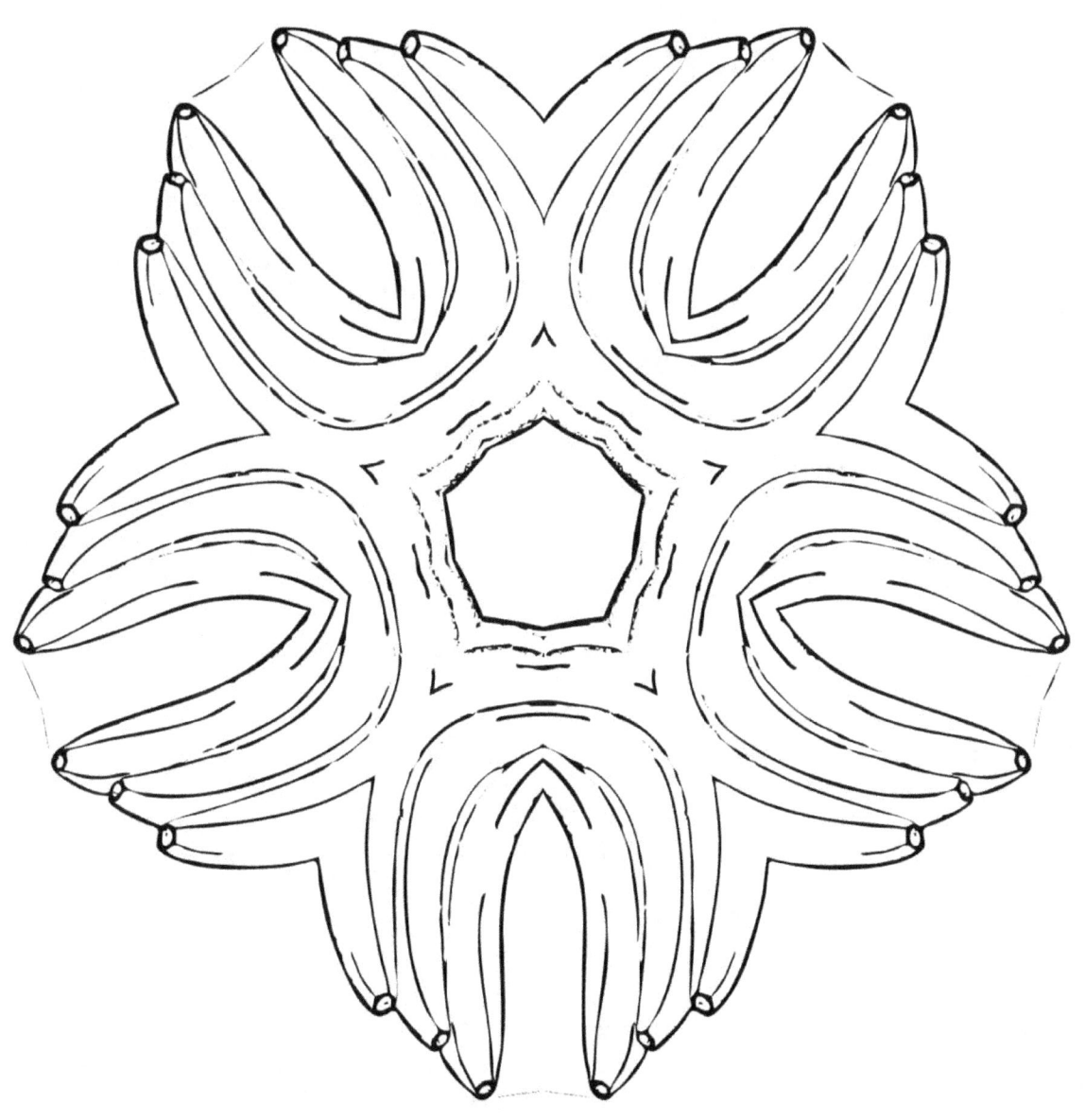

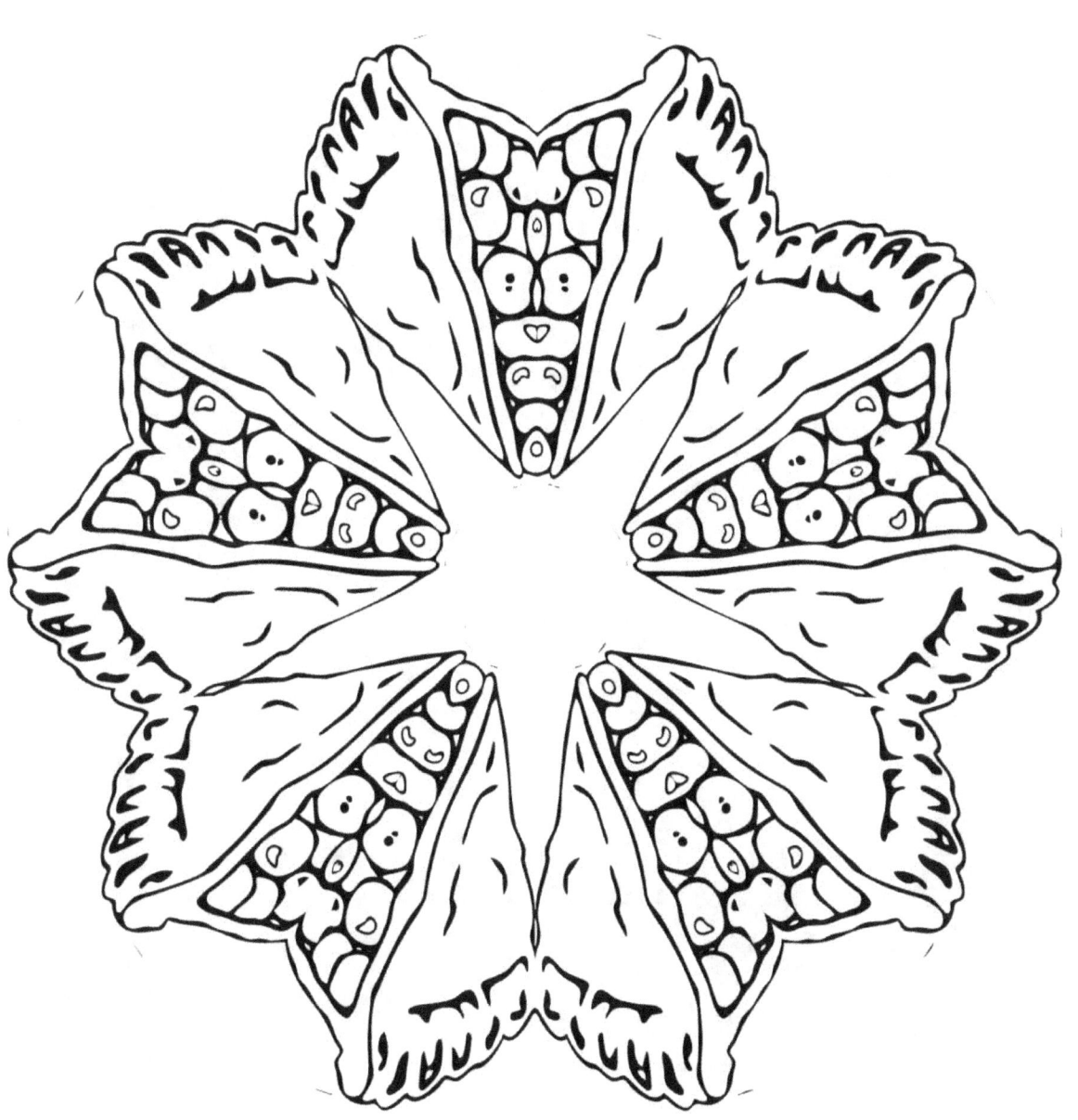

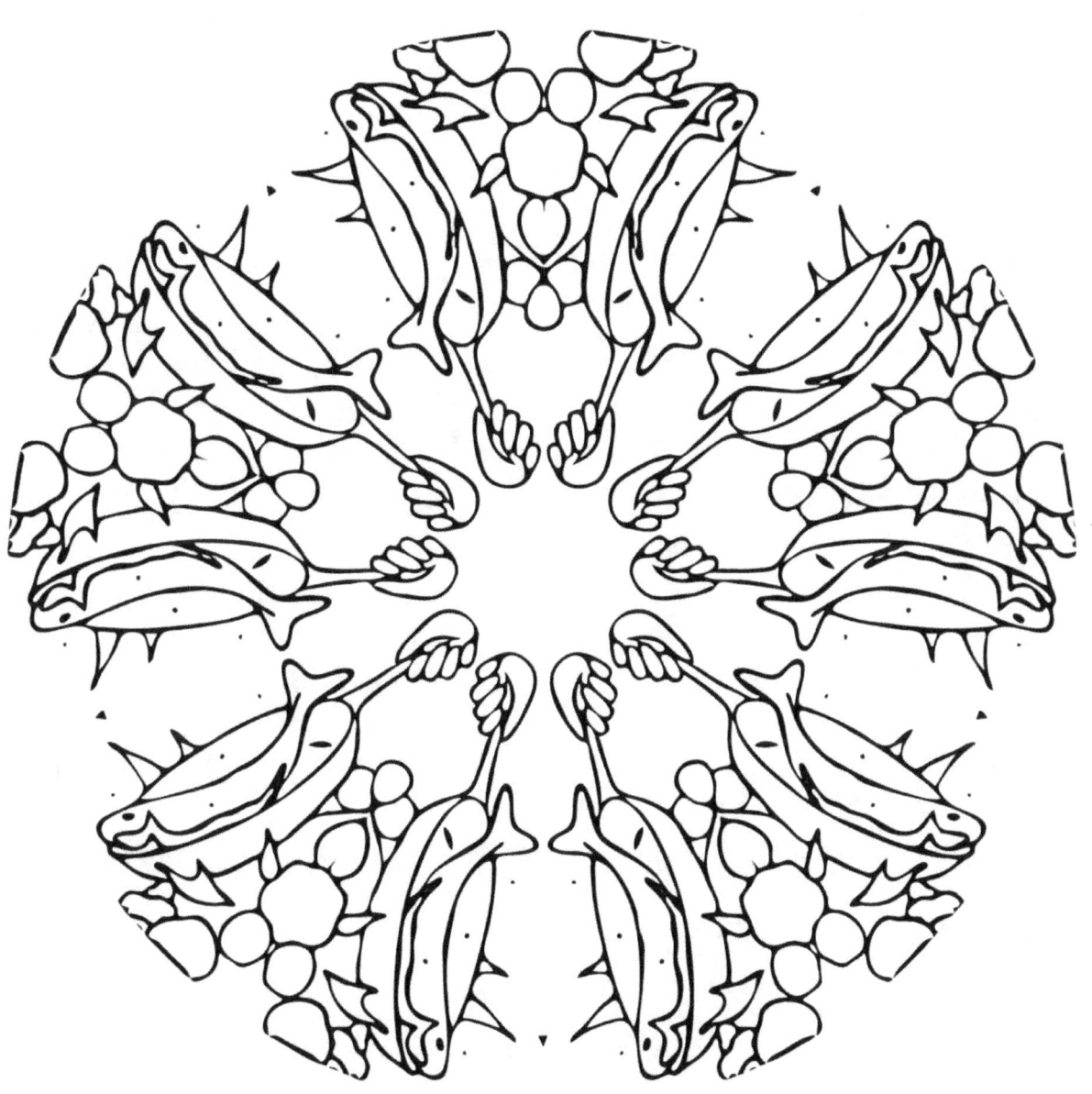

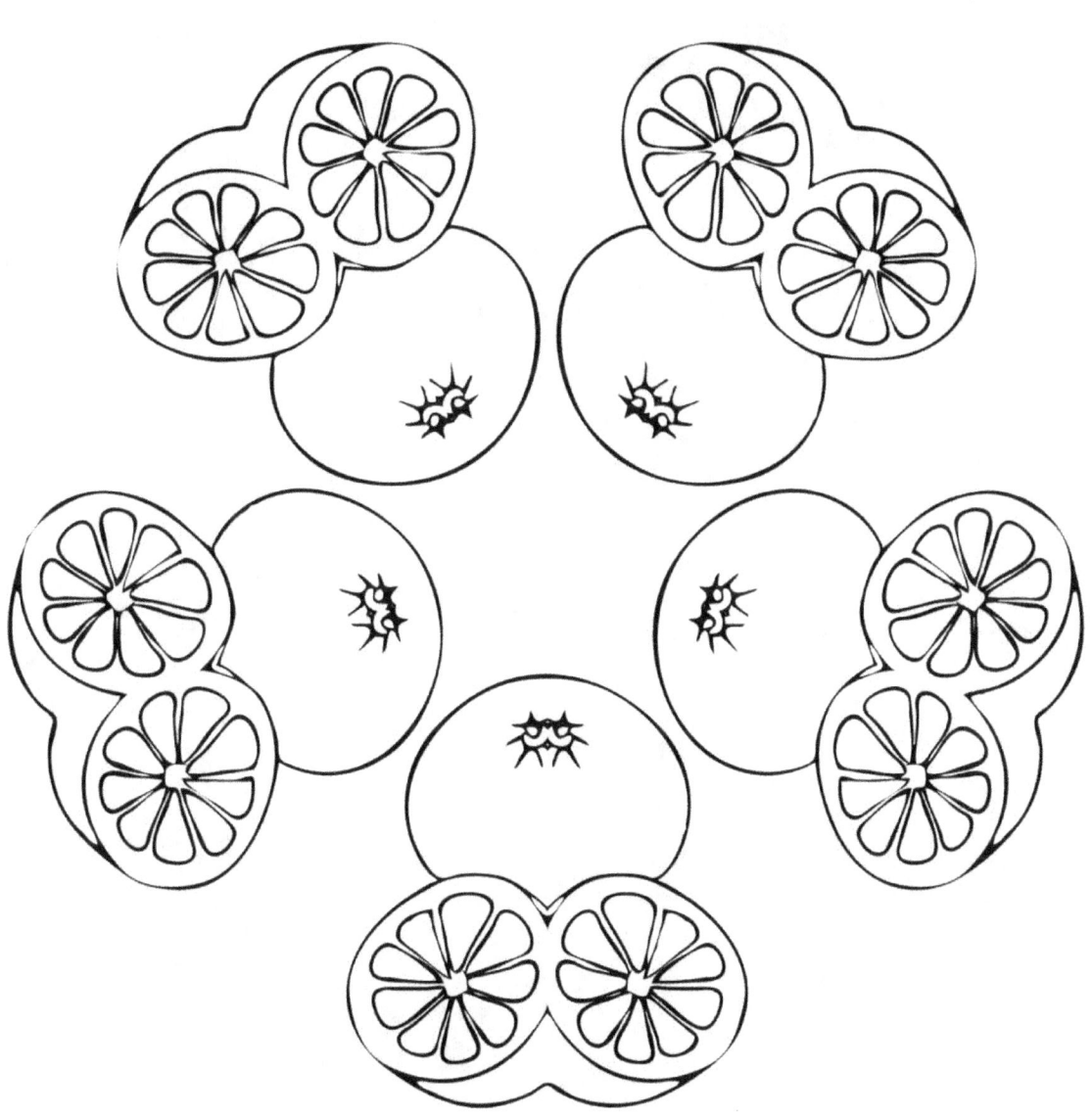

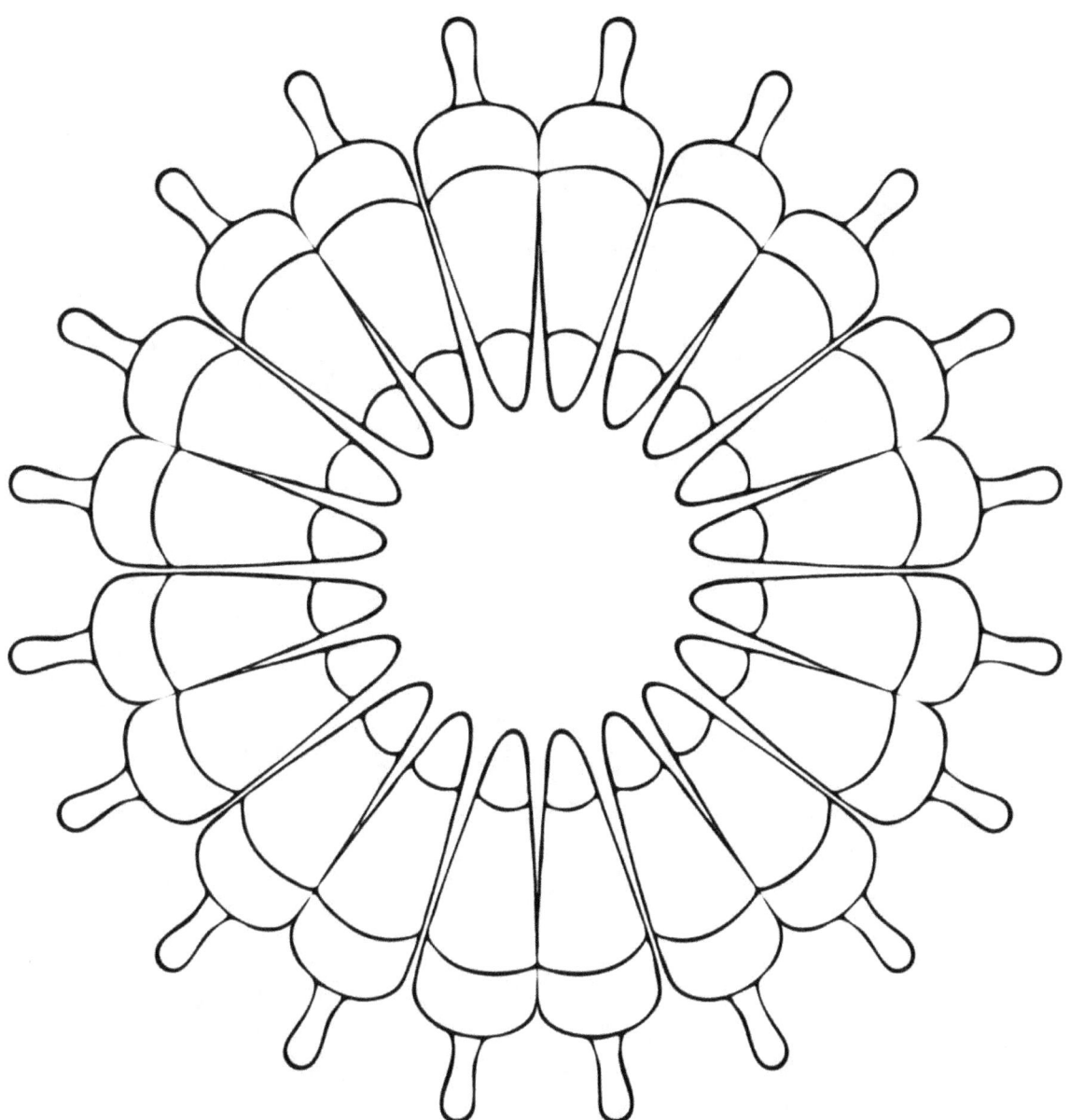

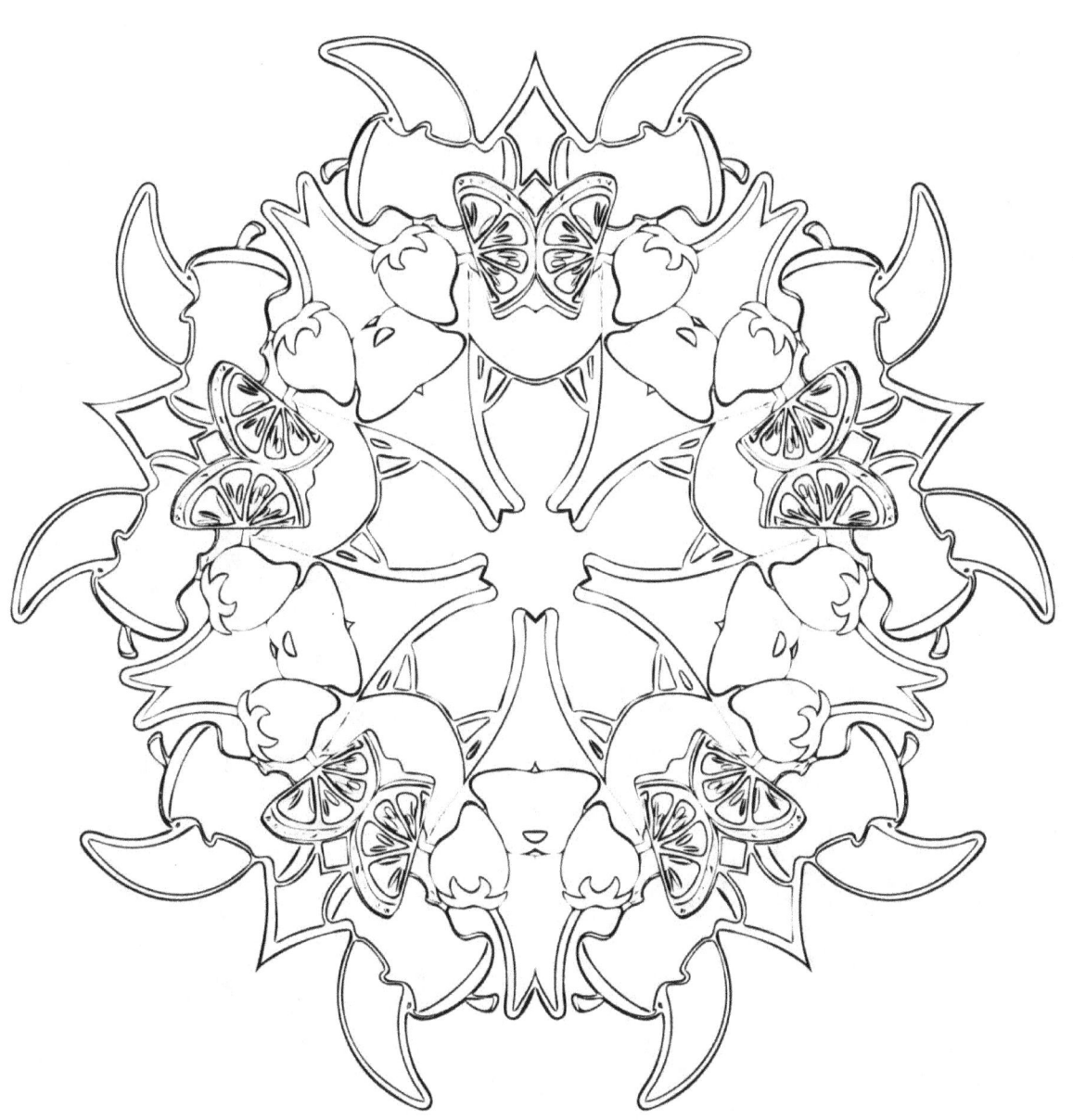

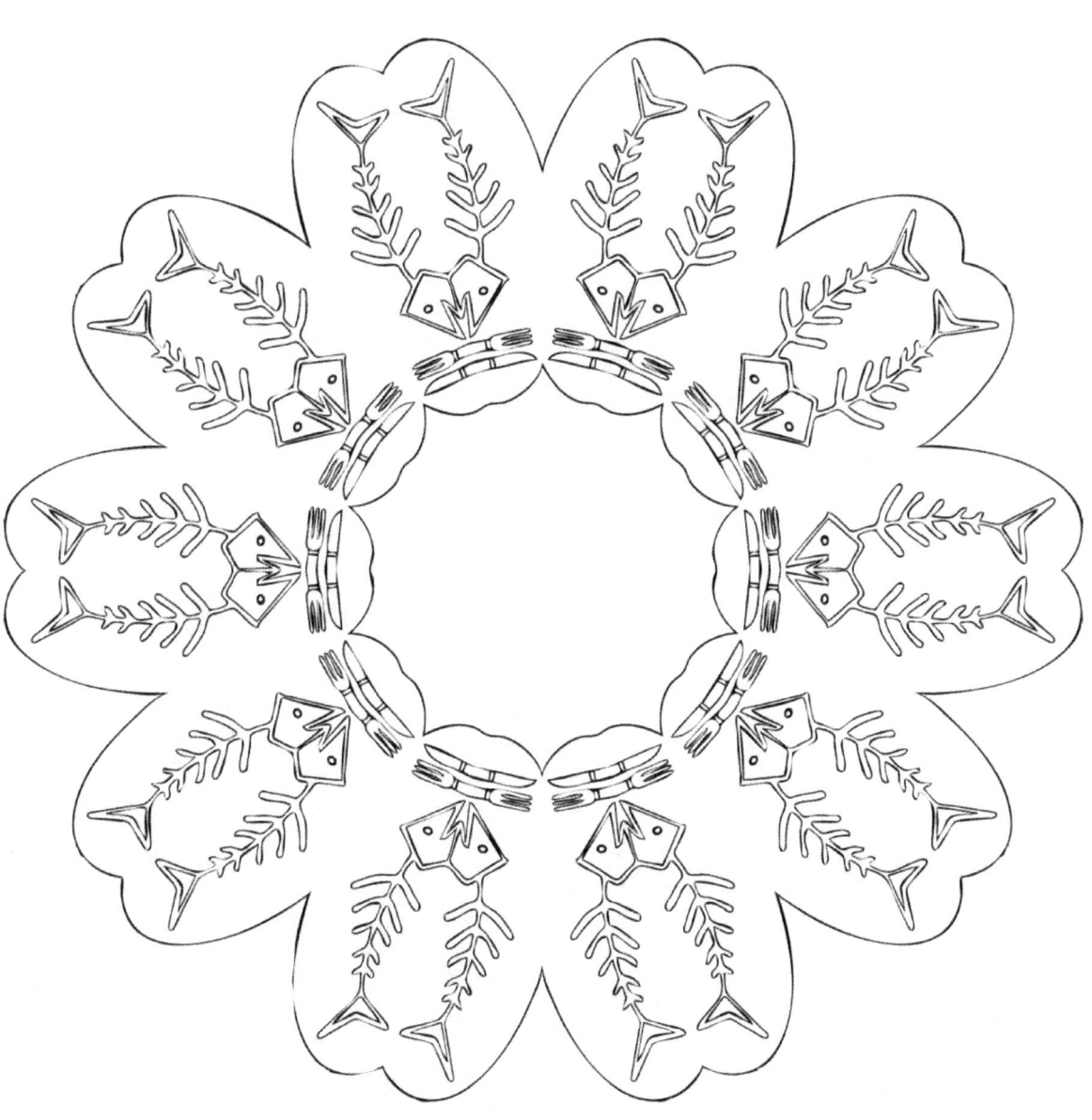

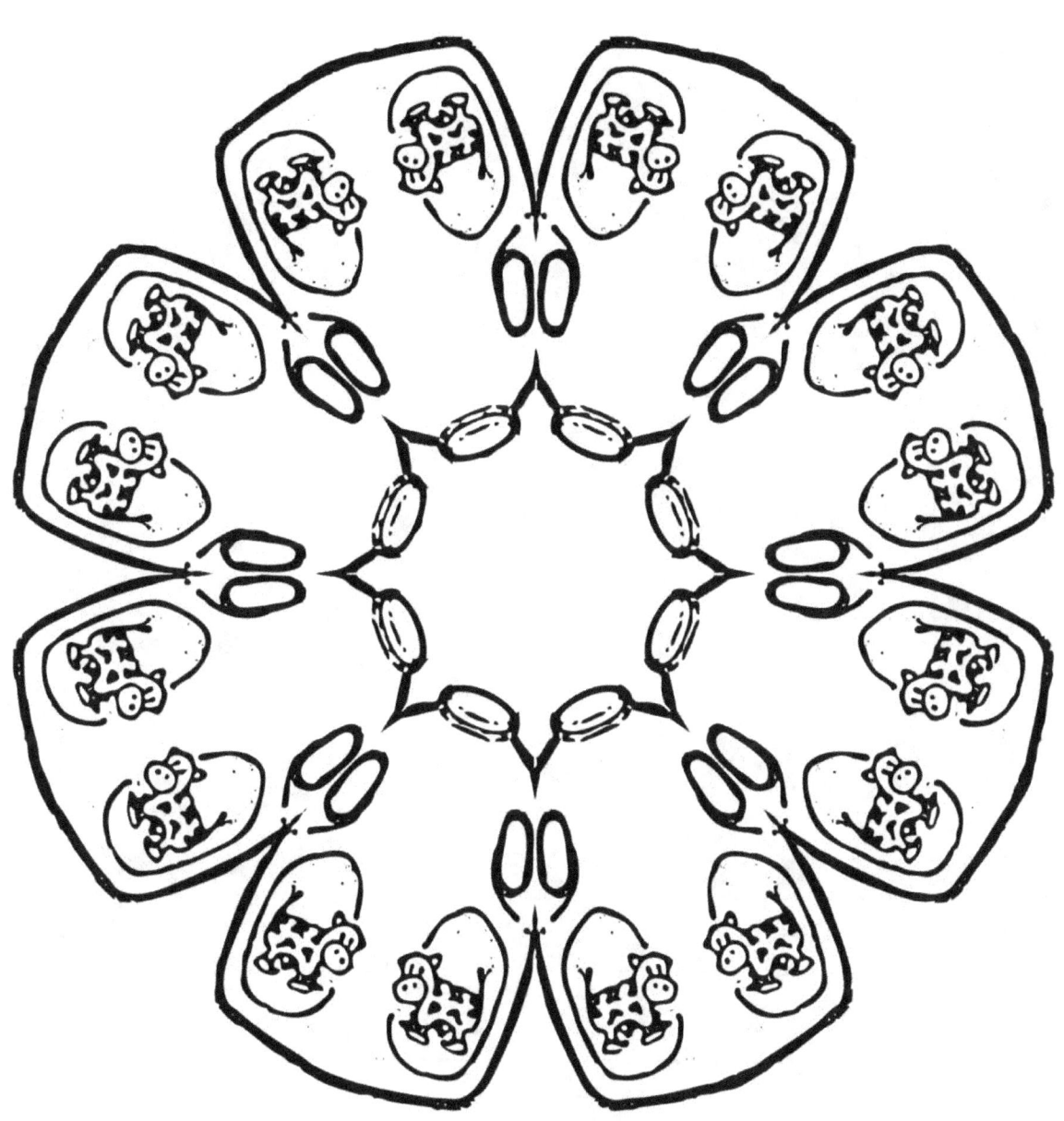

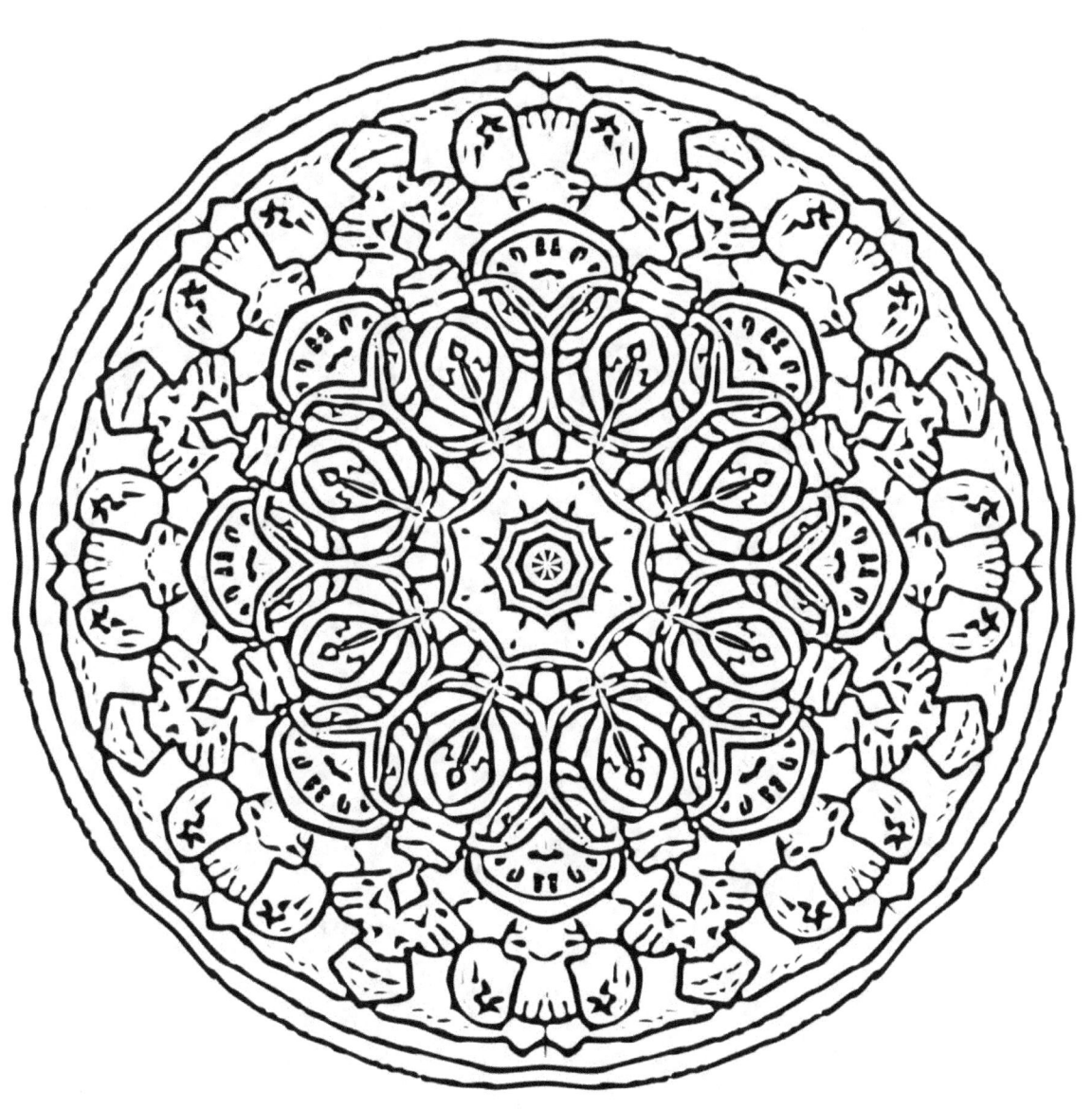

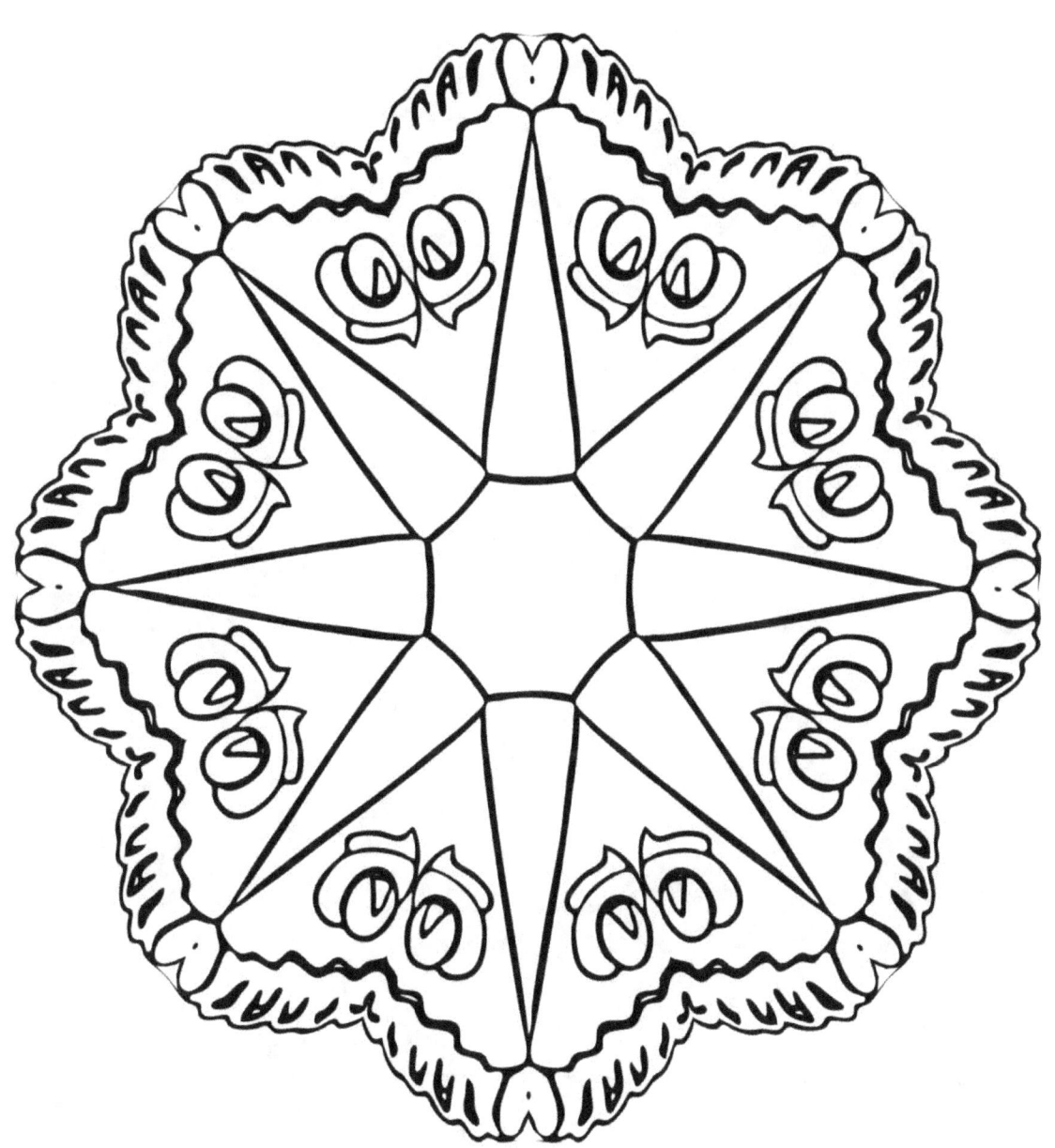

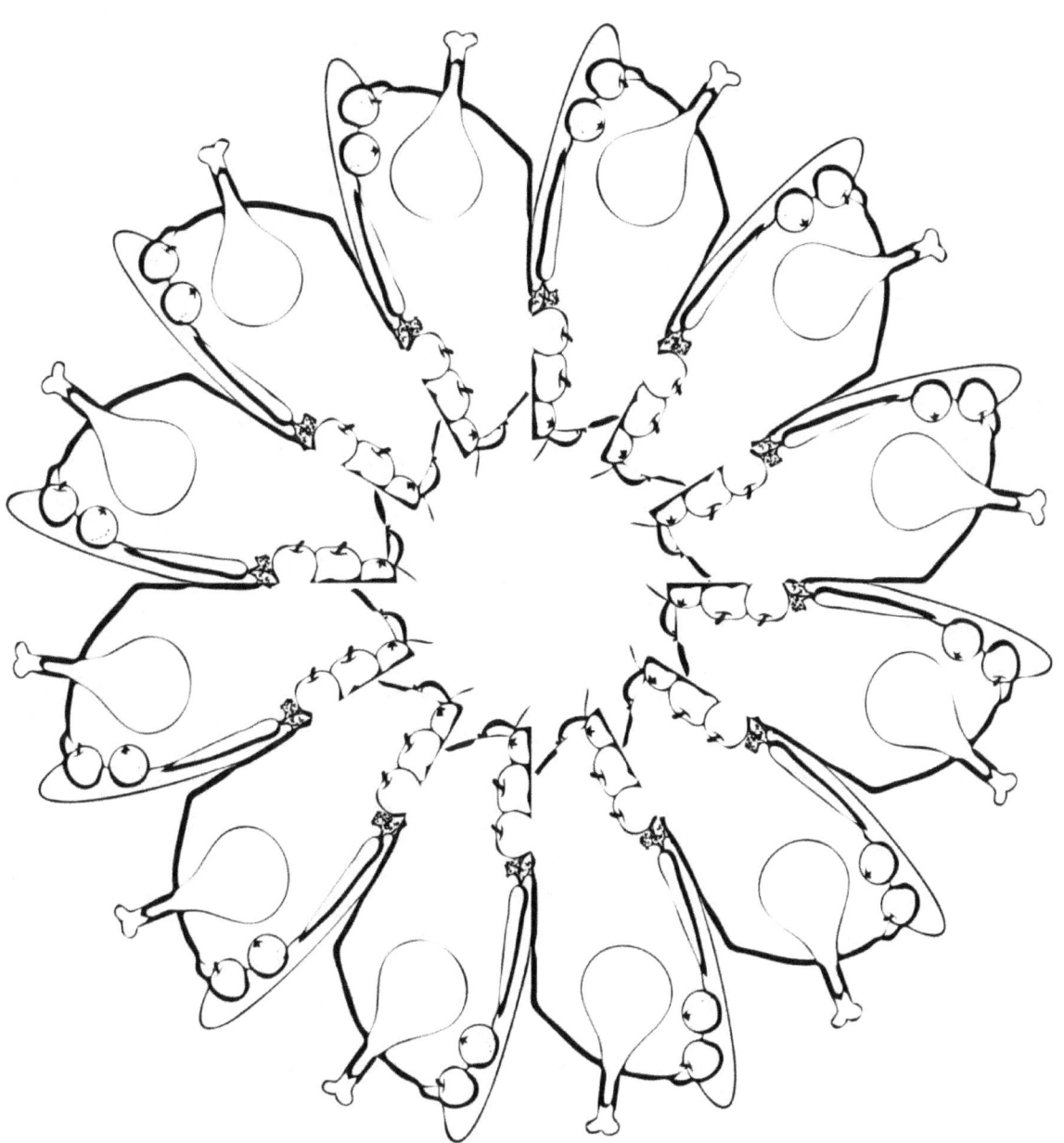

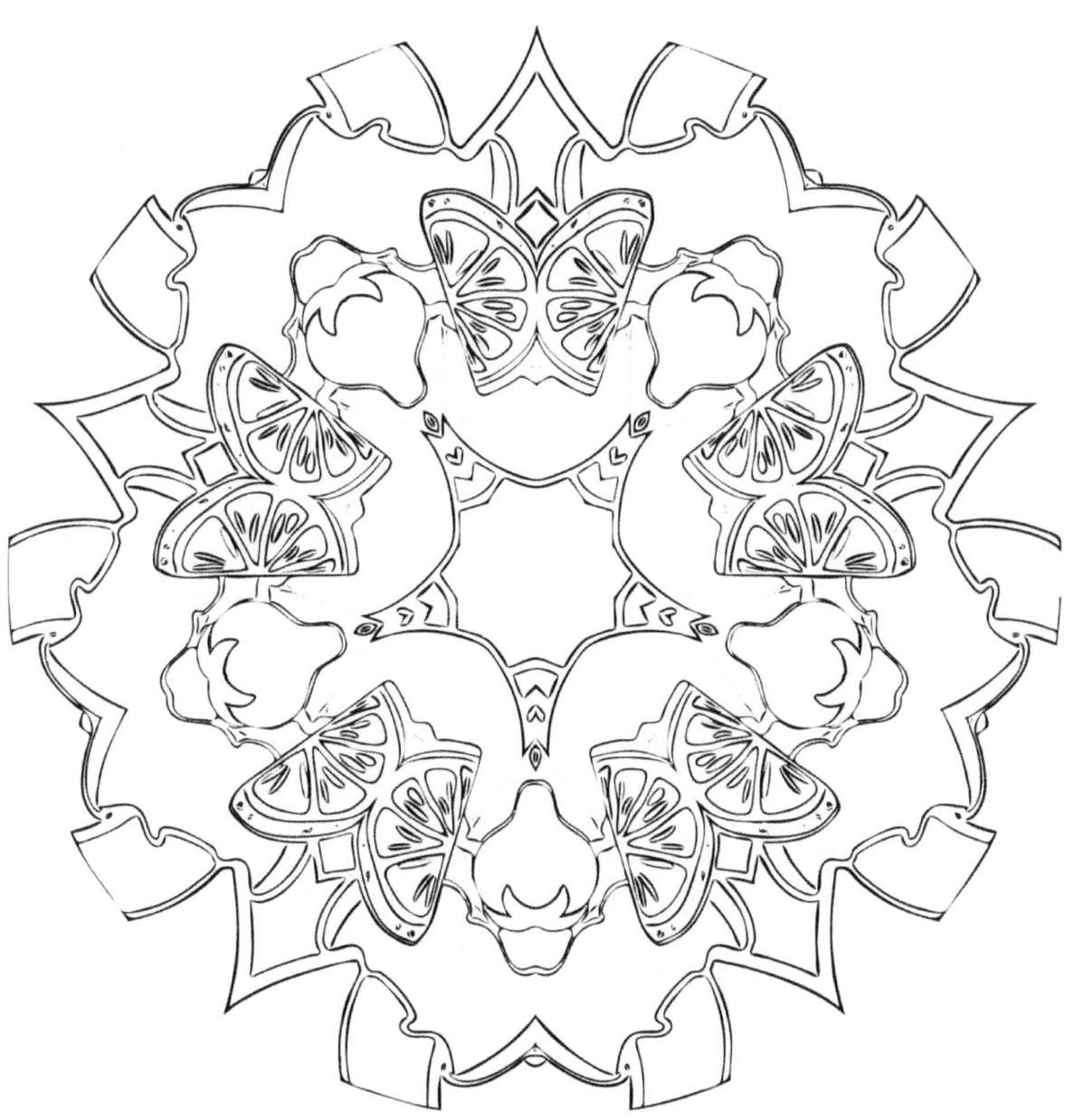

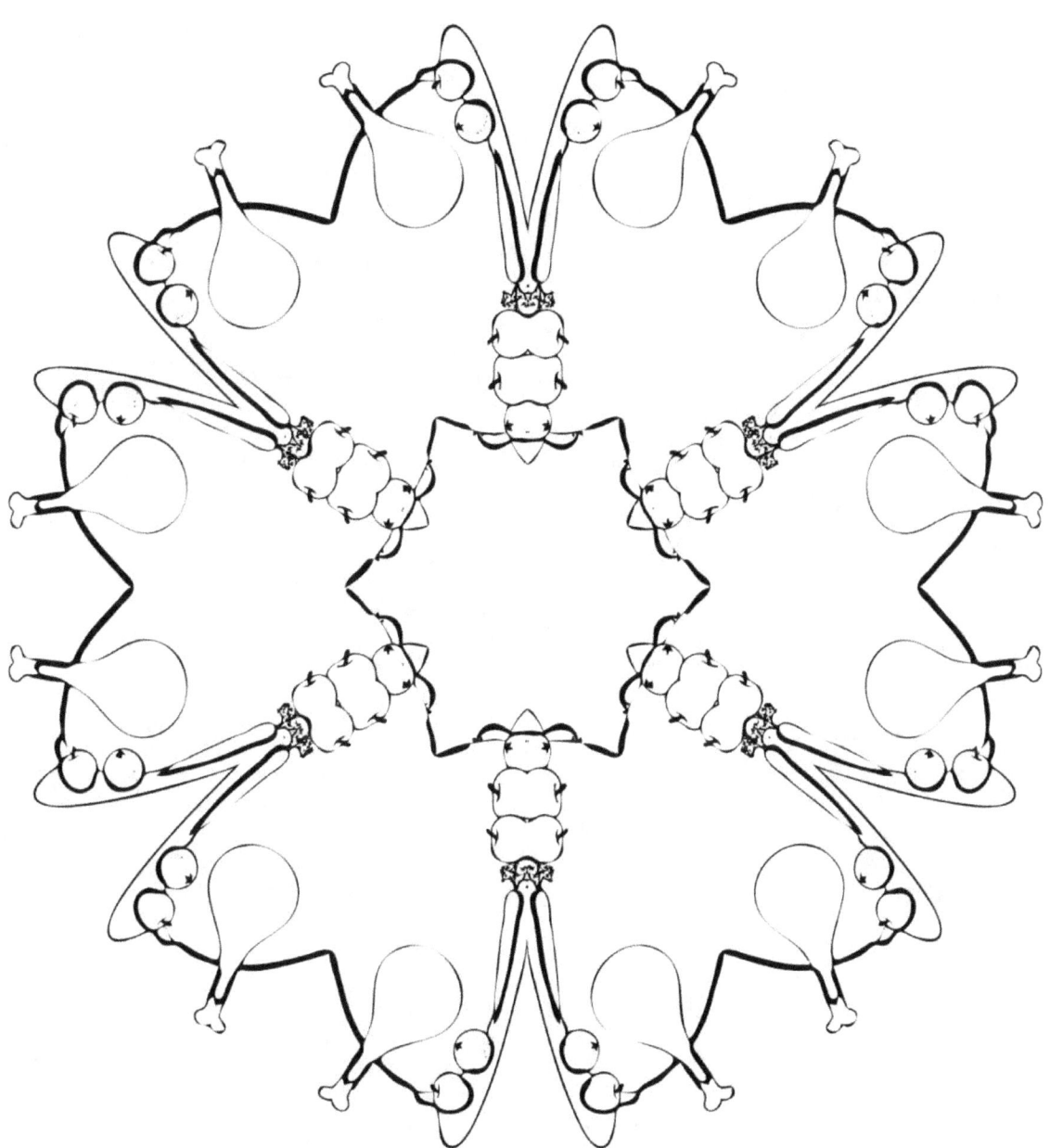

www.ingramcontent.com/pod-product-compliance
Lightning Source LLC
Chambersburg PA
CBHW081548170526
45166CB00009B/2622